The STOP Program

Innovative Skills, Techniques, Options, and Plans for Better Relationships

HANDOUTS & HOMEWORK

FOURTH EDITION

David B. Wexler

W. W. NORTON & COMPANY
Independent Publishers Since 1923

Note to Readers: Standards of clinical practice and protocol change over time, and no technique or recommendation is guaranteed to be safe or effective in all circumstances. This volume is intended as a general information resource for professionals practicing in the field of psychotherapy and mental health; it is not a substitute for appropriate training, peer review, and/or clinical supervision. Neither the publisher nor the author(s) can guarantee the complete accuracy, efficacy, or appropriateness of any particular recommendation in every respect.

All material in this book is protected by copyright. To reproduce or adapt it, in whole or in part, for any purpose whatsoever, by any means, including photocopying, reprinting, or any form of computer storage or programming, is not only a violation of copyright law, but is unethical and unprofessional. Thank you for your cooperation in complying with these standards.

Copyright © 2020, 2013, 2006, 2000 by David B. Wexler

Previous editions published under the titles DV 2000 and THE STOP PROGRAM

All rights reserved
Printed in the United States of America

For information about permission to reproduce selections from this book, write to
Permissions, W. W. Norton & Company, Inc., 500 Fifth Avenue, New York, NY 10110

For information about special discounts for bulk purchases, please contact
W. W. Norton Special Sales at specialsales@wwnorton.com or 800-233-4830

Manufacturing by Sheridan Books
Production manager: Katelyn Mackenzie

ISBN: 978-0-393-71459-3 (pbk.)

W. W. Norton & Company, Inc., 500 Fifth Avenue, New York, N.Y. 10110
www.wwnorton.com

W. W. Norton & Company Ltd., 15 Carlisle Street, London W1D 3BS

2 3 4 5 6 7 8 9 0

Contents

Welcome   v

Part I: Orientation Information

The STOP Program Q&A   3
Typical Questions and Concerns   6
Provisional Status Policy (Group Members' Version)   7
The 15 Commandments of STOP   8
Gratitudes   9
Mindfulness in Everyday Life   10
Feelings Count   12

Part II: New Member Sessions

House of Abuse   15
Time-Out   16
Time-Out Information for Partners   18
When Your Partner Blocks Your Path   19

Part III: Core Curriculum

The Cycle of Abuse   23
The Red Flags of Anger   24
The Four-Square Technique   25
Power & Control Wheel   27
Threats & Intimidation   28
Bad Rap Worksheet   30
Bad Rap   31
Bad Rap Quiz   32
Examples of Anger-Producing Self-Talk   33
Men Are Supposed To . . .   35
Masculinity Traps   36
Guidelines for Good Men   38
Jealousy   40
Misinterpretations   42
Normative Male Alexithymia   44
Anger Is A Secondary Emotion   45
Switch!   47
Put-downs from Parents   49
The Male Shame Manifesto   51
The Broken Mirror Sequence   53

Relational Heroism 54
Adverse Childhood Experiences (ACE) Info 56
What's My ACE Score? 57
ACE RESILIENCE Questionnaire 59
Assertiveness 64
What Is Assertive Behavior? 65
Asking for Change 66
Expressing Your Feelings 69
Active Listening 70
The Five Love Languages 74
Four Horsemen of the Apocalypse 78
Emotional Abuse & Mind Games 79
Conflict with Respect 81
Relationship Respect Contract 82
Which Attachment Style Am I? 84
Can I Count on You? 87
Effective Communication 88
The Art of Apologies 92
Classic Apology Mistakes 94
Handling Criticism: Nondefensive Listening 95
Sexual Abuse: Psychological & Physical 98
Masculinity Traps: Sex 100
About Sex 101
Questions for Kids 103
Accountability Statement 105
Accountability Defenses 106
The Way Aggressive People Think 107
Accountability Checklist 109
Stake In Conformity: Protect What You've Earned! 111
Screw You! 112
The MAST Assessment 113
I Really Didn't Mean to Do It . . . I Was Drunk 116
Why Do We Care?: The Relationship Between Substance Abuse And Intimate Partner Violence 117
Safe at Home Questionnaire, Revised 118
The Five Stages of Change 122
Making Changes, Pros and Cons 123
Prevention Plan 125

Part IV: Exit/Relapse Prevention Sessions

Most Violent and/or Most Disturbing Incident 129
Prevention Plan 130

Part V: Standard Forms

Weekly Check-In 133
Evaluation Form 135
Treatment Expectations 137

WELCOME

Welcome to The STOP Program. You are here because of a report indicating that you were involved in an incident of relationship violence. This destructive behavior has damaged other people close to you (emotionally and/or physically)—and it has been damaging to you as well. Even though your partner or other people in your life may have acted destructively as well, our focus in this program is on the one person over whom you have control: yourself.

This program will help you discover how abusive patterns in your most intimate relationships began—and it will help you develop new ways of dealing with the beliefs and emotions that have triggered these behaviors.

The STOP Program should really be called the "GO" program—because it is designed to move forward with something better and new, not just stop the destructive and old.

Some of the issues are difficult to face, but The STOP Program will help you deal with these problems in a supportive learning environment.

That's what real men do.

The STOP Program demands that men examine the dominance and control aspects of domestic violence—especially issues of male intimidation and entitlement. It offers men intensive training in new skills for self-management, communication, problem-solving, and empathy for others. Special attention is paid to the self-talk that determine emotions and behaviors in any given situation.

But, most importantly, The STOP Program group leaders consistently use an approach that emphasizes respect for men's experiences—both in personal history and in present relationships. The group leaders will always try to be compassionate and understanding about why you choose to act the way you do.

In a series of weekly groups, you and the other men in your group will have a chance to discuss family problems, feelings that led to destructive behaviors, and the impact violence has had on your relationships. We strongly emphasize new ways of communicating, handling stress, and resolving conflicts. Each session is designed to focus on a particular aspect of family violence. At each session your group leaders will assign exercises, handouts, and homework, which are included here.

This model has been carefully constructed through a long process of trial-and-error with thousands of men and through paying attention to new research in the field. We would like to thank all the men who have given so much of themselves and worked so hard throughout the years during which we have been developing the program. We have found that domestic violence has many causes and consequences and that each man has a unique story to tell.

Although many of the group sessions involve learning specific skills such as stress management and improved communication, the groups are considered to be "group counseling." This means that we encourage you to think about your own life, discuss your feelings, and offer support for other group members. You will get from this program what you put into it. Use your time well.

The STOP Program

Handouts & Homework

PART I
ORIENTATION INFORMATION

THE STOP PROGRAM Q&A

◆◆◆ Handout

Welcome to the STOP Program. The following is a list of answers to frequently asked questions about the groups. Please read this information carefully.

You were referred to this program because of reports that you were involved in one or more incidents of relationship violence. The fact that you have been referred indicates that this problem is treatable.

2. *How often does the group meet?*
   Each group typically meets once a week for 2 hours.

3. *Who else is in the group?*
   The group members include men like yourself who have been involved in some sort of relationship violence. This is an ongoing, open-ended group. It is very valuable to have group members at different stages of treatment to help explain to you how the group works.

4. *What happens in the group?*
   Our philosophy is that men who get into trouble in their relationships need to learn new skills. We want to make sure that you have new ways of handling stress, new ways of thinking about difficult relationship situations, and new ways of problem solving. When you leave this program, you should have lots of new tools to help you handle things differently. This will make it much less likely that the same problems will take place.

   Each session is designed to focus on a particular aspect of relationship health and/or relationship violence. Groups provide an environment in which you can discuss the problems and feelings that have led to destructive behavior and the impact violence has had on your relationship. New ways of understanding yourself, understanding others, and relating to other people are strongly emphasized.

5. *Is this a class or group counseling?*
   Although many of the group sessions involve teaching of specific skills, such as stress management and improved communication, the groups are considered to be group counseling. This means that strong emphasis is placed on self-examination, discussion of feelings, and support of other group members. Most people benefit from the group based on how committed they are to engaging in these tasks.

6. *Do I have to come every week?*
   You are required to attend every week. Research indicates that there is a direct relationship between steady attendance and treatment progress. In order for you to benefit from the program, attendance must be a priority. As you become more involved in the group, you will probably find that you are motivated to attend, not only for your own benefit but also to offer support to your fellow group members.

7. *What about absences?*
   We recognize that there may be circumstances that will require you to miss a group session. If you are unable to attend a group session, please notify our staff beforehand to let us know that you will be unable to attend. Documentation of all absences is required and should be given to our staff prior to your absence. If you miss a group for unexpected reasons, please bring in documentation for the absence at the next group session. Undocumented absences will be considered unexcused.

Unexcused absences indicate a lack of interest in or commitment to changing your situation. An unexcused absence will be grounds for a report back to your probation officer or other referring agency, which may result in the termination of treatment.

8. *What happens if I arrive late?*
If a group member arrives more than 5 minutes late, he will be marked as late. Three times late is the equivalent of one unexcused absence. If a group member arrives 15 or more minutes late, he will (under no circumstances) be allowed into the group, and this will be considered an unexcused absence.

9. *Who leads the groups?*
All of the group therapists are certified domestic violence counselors who have had extensive training in treatment of relationship violence.

10. *Are there additional expectations for successful participation other than group attendance?*
All sessions have homework assignments, which you will be expected to complete and bring to the next group meeting. The group leaders will review the homework assignment with you at the end of each group meeting so you will know what is expected. The group leaders will also discuss the completed homework at the beginning of each group meeting. Three missed homework assignments will be considered the equivalent of one unexcused absence. This will be grounds for a report back to your probation officer, case manager, social worker, commanding officer, or other referring agency, which may result in the termination of treatment.

Group members are required to be at the meeting site 10 minutes before the meeting starts to fill out the Weekly *Check-In* questionnaire. Group will not begin until everyone has completed the questionnaire.

You will be given a *STOP Program Handouts and Homework* binder at the first group meeting. Each week, information from the binder will be discussed during the group session. You must bring your binder to each group meeting.

11. *What about confidentiality? Can what I say in the group be used against me?*
Because this treatment uses a team approach, you can assume that what you say in the group may be discussed with your probation officer, case manager, social worker, commanding officer, or other referring agency. Only information that is directly related to your treatment goals is included in these reports. Most of the personal issues and feelings discussed in the group sessions remain confidential.

In certain situations, the group leaders are obligated to report information that is revealed in the group. These reportable situations include serious threats of hurting or killing someone else, serious threats of hurting or killing yourself, new and significant reports of family violence (including incidents in which children have witnessed spousal abuse), child abuse, or elder abuse.

12. *What about new incidents of violence in my relationship?*
As a participant in domestic violence treatment you are expected to discuss any new incidents of violence in your relationships. Presenting such information does not necessarily lead to termination if you genuinely appear to be remorseful, take responsibility for your actions, and appear to be making efforts to prevent a similar reoccurrence in the future. Keep in mind that it is in your best interest to disclose a new incident of violence. When these incidents are discovered through other sources, it reflects negatively on you.

13. *What about electronic devices?*
    Please turn off all electronic devices during group sessions. You will have an opportunity at the break to reply to text or phone messages.

14. *How should I dress for the group?*
    There is no specific dress code. However, clothing with inappropriate messages, promoting or making light of sexism or violence, or displaying otherwise inappropriate content will not be permitted.

15. *Any other rules about appropriate behavior?*
    While you are in your group, you are asked to use respectful language that is not offensive to staff or other group members.

    You may not use alcohol or drugs prior to the group session.

    Group members will not threaten or intimidate the group or leaders at any time.

    I have read the above information and agree to the conditions of treatment.

    _____   _____
    Group Member's Signature   Print Name

    _____   _____
    Date   Group Name

TYPICAL QUESTIONS AND CONCERNS

◆◆◆ Handout

1. *Won't group counseling try and get me to let out all my emotions? I'm not comfortable with that!*
   Everybody in group counseling is different, and each person decides how much of his personal emotions to reveal to others. No one is expected to walk right in and talk about their deepest feelings in front of a bunch of strangers.

   Over time, most people become more and more comfortable letting the group know more about what is happening inside. We know that there is usually a correlation between talking about yourself and getting some benefit from the sessions. But this all happens at the pace of the individual.

2. *I would rather have individual counseling because I don't like talking in front of other people and I can get more personal attention.*
   The STOP Program philosophy is that these kinds of problems are best treated in a group setting. You get the benefit of hearing about the experiences of others and learning from their successes and mistakes. The feedback from peers is one of the single most important factors in predicting positive outcome.

3. *I don't want to be in a group with a bunch of spouse abusers—I'm not like them!*
   We treat the man, not the label. We stay away from labels that sound like put-downs. Instead, we focus on the specific thoughts, feelings, and situations that have led to problem behaviors. We could put any man in this group, regardless of what has gone wrong in his behavior with others, and he would benefit from the approaches used in this treatment model.

PROVISIONAL STATUS POLICY (GROUP MEMBERS' VERSION)

Handout

The following—in addition to activity that takes place outside of the group sessions, such as acts of violence, repeated drug or alcohol problems, or failure to attend group—are grounds for group members to be placed on provisional status in the STOP Program (leading to possible termination):

1. **Consistent** put-downs of women or minimization of violence
2. **Persistent** disruptive or oppositional behavior in group
3. **Consistent** projection of blame for relationship problems without self-examination
4. **Consistent** lack of participation in group, including failure to complete homework assignments
5. **Consistent** pattern of "telling stories" (bragging or showing off) about controlling, abusive, or violent behavior, with few or no signs of remorse
6. **Consistent** pattern of inappropriate messages on clothing (such as T-shirts with sexist messages)

THE 15 COMMANDMENTS OF STOP

Handout

1. We are all 100% responsible for our own actions (even when it feels like someone else made us do it).
2. Violence is not an acceptable solution to problems.
3. Anger is normal. Being consumed by anger, or being driven to commit acts of aggression or retaliation because of anger, is not. It is your responsibility to recognize this and take action to stop it.
4. Recognize that anger is—always—a secondary emotion. Identify the primary one first, and you are really in a position of power.
5. We do not have control over any other person, but we do have control over ourselves.
6. We can always take a Time-Out before reacting.
7. We can't do anything about the past, but we can change the future.
8. Self-talk is everything. We are always telling ourselves stories about the events in our world—and the stories can always change.
9. Sometimes anger can be very quiet and cold. Just because you are not yelling—even if you are smiling—does not mean that you are not being aggressive.
10. Just because someone "deserves" retaliation doesn't mean that retaliating is wise, productive, or moral to deliver it.
11. When you let go of anger, you are doing yourself a big favor. You are no longer allowing the situation or the person to control you.
12. Use gratitudes whenever you need to, and appreciate the power and positivity they will confer on you.
13. Always have a Prevention Plan in your back pocket. And remember the big picture.
14. Although there are differences between men and women, our needs and rights are fundamentally alike.
15. Counselors and case managers cannot make people change—they can only set the stage for change to occur.

GRATITUDES

❖ Handout

The Upward Spiral (Korb, 2015)

- Does gratitude really affect your brain at the biological level? *YES!*
- The antidepressant Wellbutrin boosts the neurotransmitter called dopamine. *So does gratitude.*
- Prozac boosts the neurotransmitter called serotonin. *So does gratitude.*
- It's not the finding of gratitude that matters most; it's remembering to look in the first place. Remembering to be grateful is a form of emotional intelligence.
- And gratitude doesn't just make your brain happy—it can also create a positive feedback loop in your relationships. So, express that gratitude to the people you care about.

It's not happiness that brings us gratitude. It's gratitude that bring us happiness.

People who keep a list of a few things they are grateful for each day . . .

- exercise more/feel more energy and vitality;
- are less bothered by pain;
- sleep thirty minutes more each night;
- feel closer and more connected to others;
- report greater well-being and optimism;
- report more attentiveness, enthusiasm and determination;
- cope better with situations that might have made them angry.

Think of one person who has been very important in your life. Write down the three most important things that this person has done for you.

Here are some examples of things that might happen in your life in a typical week that are worthy of gratitude:

- *I had a great conversation with my wife last night—I used what we learned in the group, and she said it was one of the best conversations we've ever had. I am so grateful.*
- *I talked to a friend of mine and helped him out with a problem. I am grateful that I got a chance to do that.*
- *Somebody at work here really took one of my concerns seriously and followed through on it. I am really grateful.*
- *I watched my kids playing together last night, and they were really getting along. I really felt lucky.*

MINDFULNESS IN EVERYDAY LIFE

Handout

Mindfulness is a form of self-awareness training: a state of being *in the present* and *accepting things for what they are* (non-judgmentally).

Just observe whatever happens. Label any thoughts (*oh, there goes a "worried" thought*) and then leave them alone--just be prepared to let them float away. Pay attention to your breathing or simply notice your surroundings instead.

When emotions or memories show up, just give them labels like *that's a sad feeling or that's an angry feeling*—and then just allow them to drift away. These memories and feelings will gradually decrease in intensity and frequency.

ONE-MINUTE MINDFULNESS TECHNIQUES

- Focus your entire attention on your breath just coming in and out, and nothing else, for one minute
- Chew on a raisin for one minute, paying full attention to the taste and texture of this experience
- Walk across a small room, taking a full minute to take the steps, focusing on all the sensations and feelings in your body as you move so slowly
- Pick a spot on the wall across from you and focus all of your attention on that spot for one minute
- Invent your own!!!!

EXTENDED MINDFULNESS EXERCISES

Follow Your Breath While Listening to Music. Listen to a piece of music. Breathe long, light, and even breaths. Follow your breath; be aware of it while remaining aware of the sound of the music. Don't get lost in the music—just continue to be aware of your breath and yourself.

Making Tea or Coffee. Prepare a pot of tea or coffee to serve a guest or to drink by yourself. Do each movement slowly, in awareness. Pay attention to pouring the warm tea or coffee into the cup. Breathe gently and more deeply than usual. Take hold of your breath in your mind strays.

Chopping Vegetables. Pay full attention to the colors and textures of the vegetables. Feel the weight and balance of the knife in your hands. Pay attention to the slicing motion—and nothing else. Keep your breathing slow and regular throughout.

Washing Dishes. Wash the dishes consciously, as though each plate or utensil is an object of contemplation. Don't hurry to get the job over with--just for this moment, consider washing the dishes the most important thing in life.

Taking A Shower. From the moment you turn in the shower to the moment you put on clothes, be attentive to every movement. Be aware of each stream of water on your body.

Eating. This involves sitting down at a table and eating a meal without engaging in any other activities—no newspaper, book, TV, radio, music, or talking. Now eat your meal paying full attention to which piece of food you select to eat, how it looks, how it smells, how you cut the food, the muscles you use to raise it to your mouth, the texture and taste of the food as you chew it slowly. You may be amazed at how different food tastes when eaten in this way and how filling a meal can be. It is also very good for the digestion.

Mindful Walking. The same principle: while walking, you concentrate on the feel of the ground under your feet, and your breathing while walking. Just observe what is around you as you walk, staying IN THE PRESENT. Let your other thoughts go, just look at the sky, the view, the other walkers; feel the wind, the temperature on your skin; enjoy the moment.

Adapted from Nhat Hanh, T. (1987) and from http://www.blackdoginstitute.org.au

FEELINGS COUNT

Handout

HAPPY AND CONFIDENT

Accepted	Alive	Brave	Calm	Caring	Cheerful
Comfortable	Confident	Excited	Friendly	Fulfilled	Generous
Grateful	Happy	Hopeful	Joyful	Lovable	Loving
Peaceful	Playful	Powerful	Proud	Relaxed	Relieved
Respected	Secure	Understood	Valuable	Warm	
Worthwhile					

FEAR AND WORRY

Anxious	Apprehensive	Confused	Desperate	Distrustful
Fearful	Helpless	Horrified	Inhibited	Out-of-Control
Trapped	Panicky	Pressured	Threatened	Overwhelmed
Troubled	Uncertain	Uneasy	Uptight	Vulnerable
Worried				

ANGRY AND RESENTFUL

Angry	Bitter	Contemptuous	Disgusted	Disrespected
Frustrated	Furious	Hostile	Impatient	Irritated
Outraged	Provoked	Resentful	Stubborn	Unappreciated
Used	Victimized			

SAD AND PESSIMISTIC

Confused	Defeated	Depressed	Devastated	Disappointed
Discouraged	Helpless	Hopeless	Isolated	Lonely
Miserable	Trapped	Sad	Stuck	Overwhelmed
Useless				

UNCOMFORTABLE AND INSECURE

Awkward	Embarrassed	Foolish	Humiliated	Inhibited
Insecure	Self-conscious	Shy	Uncomfortable	

APOLOGETIC AND GUILTY

Apologetic	Guilty	Remorseful	Sorry	Untrustworthy

HURT AND REJECTED

Devastated	Excluded	Hurt	Ignored	Rejected	Vulnerable

JEALOUS AND LEFT OUT

Envious	Deprived	Left-out	Jealous

ASHAMED AND INADEQUATE

Ashamed	Inferior	Inadequate	Incompetent	Stupid
Useless	Unattractive	Unworthy	Powerless	

MAY NOT BE REPRODUCED WITHOUT PERMISSION

PART II
NEW MEMBER SESSIONS

NEW MEMBER SESSION I

THE HOUSE OF ABUSE*

◆◆◆ **Handout**

Physical Abuse	Intimidation	Child Abuse
Verbal/Emotional/Psychological		Social Isolation
Religion	Gender Privilege	Sexual Abuse

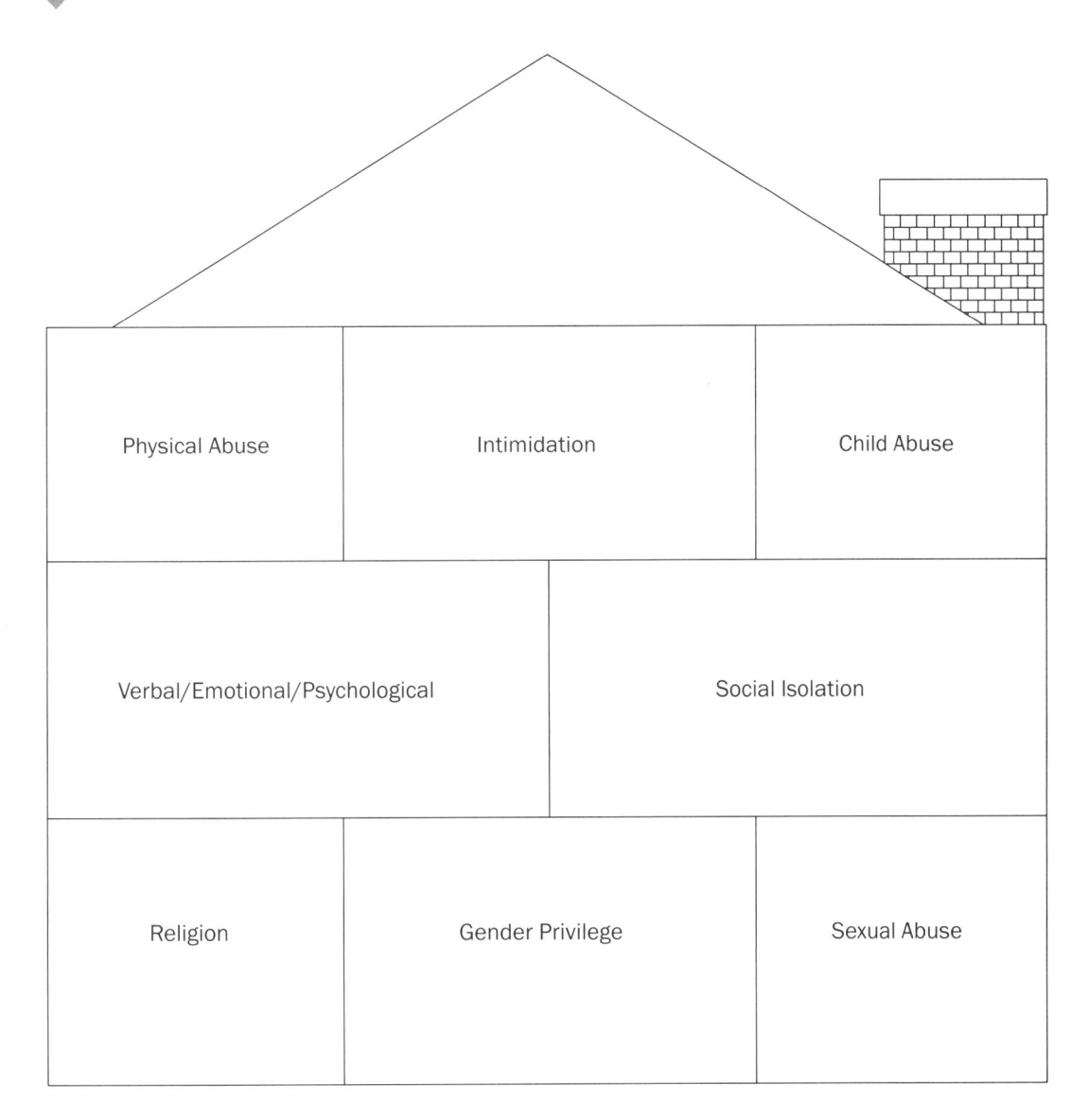

*The House of Abuse chart was developed by Michael F. McGrane, MSW, LICSW, Director of the Violence Prevention & Intervention Services (VPIS) of the Amherst H. Wilder Foundation, and is used here by permission. The chart is part of a complete domestic abuse curriculum entitled *Foundations for Violence-Free Living: A Step-by-Step Guide to Facilitating Men's Domestic Abuse Groups*, available from Fieldstone Alliance at 1-800-274-6024. May not be reproduced without permission.

NEW MEMBER SESSION II

TIME-OUT

◆◆◆ Handout

The Time-Out is an emergency strategy to prevent the dangerous escalation of conflicts. It should be used only in a crisis—and as you learn better communication and self-management skills, it may never need to be used at all. But you must know how to use it effectively.

IF YOU USE TIME-OUTS FREQUENTLY, SOMETHING IS SERIOUSLY WRONG WITH YOUR RELATIONSHIP. DO NOT TAKE A TIME-OUT SIMPLY BECAUSE YOU WISH TO AVOID TALKING ABOUT A CERTAIN SUBJECT. THIS IS FOR EMERGENCIES ONLY, AND YOU MUST BE PREPARED TO RESUME THE DISCUSSION LATER ON.

The Time-Out should not be used as a weapon against the other person. It should not be used as a way of avoiding conflicts. It should not be used as a way of making the other person feel abandoned ("I'm outta here, babe—I'll show you who's in charge!").

Instead, the Time-Out should be used as a sign of respect for the relationship. The message is this: I care enough about us that I don't want any more damage to this relationship.

It is essential that your partner understand this message of respect. It is your job to clearly explain this in advance and to follow it up with your actions by using the Time-Out correctly.

1. *I'm beginning to feel like things are getting out of control.*
2. *And I don't want to do anything that would mess up our relationship.*
3. *So I need to take a Time-Out.*
4. *I'm going out for a walk around the neighborhood (or my sister's house, or the gym, etc.).*
5. *I'll be back in (5 minutes, or 1 hour, etc.)*
6. *And let's try talking about this again when I get back. Okay?*

The partner responds:

7. *Okay. Time-Out.*

If he or she does not acknowledge, begin the Time-Out anyway—without making any physical contact or threats!

Leave silently—no door slamming.
While away, don't drink or use drugs—and don't drive if your temper is out of control.
Try using "self-talk" that will help you keep this in perspective:

- *I'm getting upset, but I don't have to lose my cool!*
- *I'm frustrated, but I don't have to control anybody else or always get my way.*
- *I can calm myself and think through this situation.*
- *I've got to think about what will be most important for the future.*

Do something physical (walking, playing sports, working out, etc.) if it will help you discharge tension. Try distracting yourself with any activity that temporarily takes your mind off the intensity of the argument.

You must come back when you said you would; otherwise, you need to call and check in.
When you come back, decide together if you want to continue the discussion. Here are the options at this point:

- **Discuss it now:** This is usually the best and most respectful action, but there are some exceptions.
- **Drop the issue:** Maybe you both realize now that it was really not that big a deal.
- **Put the issue on hold:** This may be important to discuss, but it would be better to do it later. As long as both parties agree, this can work.

Each person has the right to say "no" to further discussion at that time and to suggest a time for discussion. If anger escalates again, take another Time-Out.

TIME-OUT INFORMATION FOR PARTNERS*

◆◆◆ Handout

Please note that this form is written as if males are taking the Time-Outs and females have questions about what to do. These same instructions can, and should, apply to any partner violence, including female-to-male and between gay partners. Please change the pronouns to fit your personal situation as appropriate.

1. **How do Time-Outs help solve our family problems?**
   Your partner's use of Time-Outs will prevent him from escalating into physical or psychological abuse. Time-Outs alone do not solve destructive conflicts, but if used faithfully they will help him avoid extremely destructive behavior. Family problems have to be discussed and their solutions must be agreed upon. This cannot happen if one person is abusive of the other. No communication takes place when there is abuse. Time-Outs are a necessary first step toward respectful communication.

2. **What do I do if every time I want to discuss an important topic with my partner, he says he is taking a Time-Out?**
   Let him take the Time-Out anyway. If he becomes angry and abusive, it won't be any easier to talk about the problems. At first, he may take Time-Outs a lot. Just remind yourself that it is only one step and that he will be expected to use other approaches as well. Read the instruction sheet—it will help you understand how it works.

3. **What if he refuses to discuss the matter even after the Time-Out?**
   Notice on the instruction sheet that he has several choices as to what he does after a Time-Out. He is not supposed to drop issues if they are important to you. However, he may put them on hold until he is able to calmly speak *and* listen to you. If he refuses to discuss an issue, your insisting he does will not bring about the communication. Let him know that you are still interested in talking about the issue, but be willing to set a later time when he can be calmer when discussing it.

4. **Should I remind my partner to take a Time-Out when he is getting angry or abusive?**
   No. He is responsible for identifying his own feelings and taking the Time-Out. As long as you do it for him, he is not doing his job. If you are upset about his abuse, you could take a Time-Out for yourself, as long as you can do it safely. Remember: You cannot control another person's behavior; you can only protect yourself.

5. **What should I do when he takes a Time-Out during a discussion?**
   Remind yourself that this is the first step—that it is better for him to take a Time-Out than to be abusive toward you. Waiting for him to return can lead to your feeling frustrated or abandoned. You can use the time during a Time-Out for yourself and then go about your regular business.

6. **Would Time-Outs be useful for me?**
   Yes, if you find your own anger rising, a Time-Out is a tool you can use to calm down before you go further in working out a conflict. However, using Time-Outs for yourself will not necessarily change your partner's behaviors. Time-Outs are good for you to use when you are in conflicts with your children or with other people.

---

*Adapted with permission from the Family Violence Prevention Fund's publication entitled Domestic Violence: A National Curriculum for Family Preservation Practitioners, written by Susan Schecter, MSW, and Anne L. Ganley, PhD. May not be reproduced without permission.

WHEN YOUR PARTNER BLOCKS YOUR PATH

Handout

Sometimes, your partner will not cooperate with your attempts to take a Time-Out no matter how respectful you are. Here is a sequence that sometimes occurs:

1. You declare a Time-Out (following the steps correctly).
2. Your partner blocks your path so you cannot leave.
3. You remind her of the Time-Out agreement that you two have previously discussed.
4. She continues to block your path.
5. You offer your partner the opportunity to leave instead of you, so she does not feel abandoned by you. For example, you might say, "OK, if you want to leave, that's cool too. I don't want you to feel like I'm leaving you. We just need a break right now until things calm down."

In this situation, you cannot afford to place any hands on your partner or to use any significant force to move her. Not only is this dangerous and disrespectful, but it is very likely that YOU will be arrested.

If none of these strategies are successful in separating the two of you, you have three basic options:

1. Physical Escape

   - *Retreat through another exit (into a bathroom or a bedroom) and lock the door.*
   - *Escape through a window if it is safe to do so.*
   - *Agree to stay and discuss the situation until your partner relaxes and no longer blocks the door, then escape.*

2. Calling for Help

   - *Dial 911. Explain that your partner will not allow you to leave the premises. Make it clear that you are trying to avoid violence.*
   - *Call someone who can talk to your partner and try to calm her down to cooperate with the Time-Out.*
   - *Scream for help.*

3. Staying Put

   - *Sit down and stay quiet. Repeat self-talk to yourself, such as "It's not worth it to get into a fight" or "It's my job to stay calm now." Use relaxation techniques, such as deep breathing, to help you stay calm.*

None of these options are particularly great. They all contain significant risks, but they are designed to accomplish the most important goal in this situation: preventing both of you from getting hurt. We hope that you are never in this situation, but these are important strategies to keep in mind just in case.

PART IV
CORE CURRICULUM

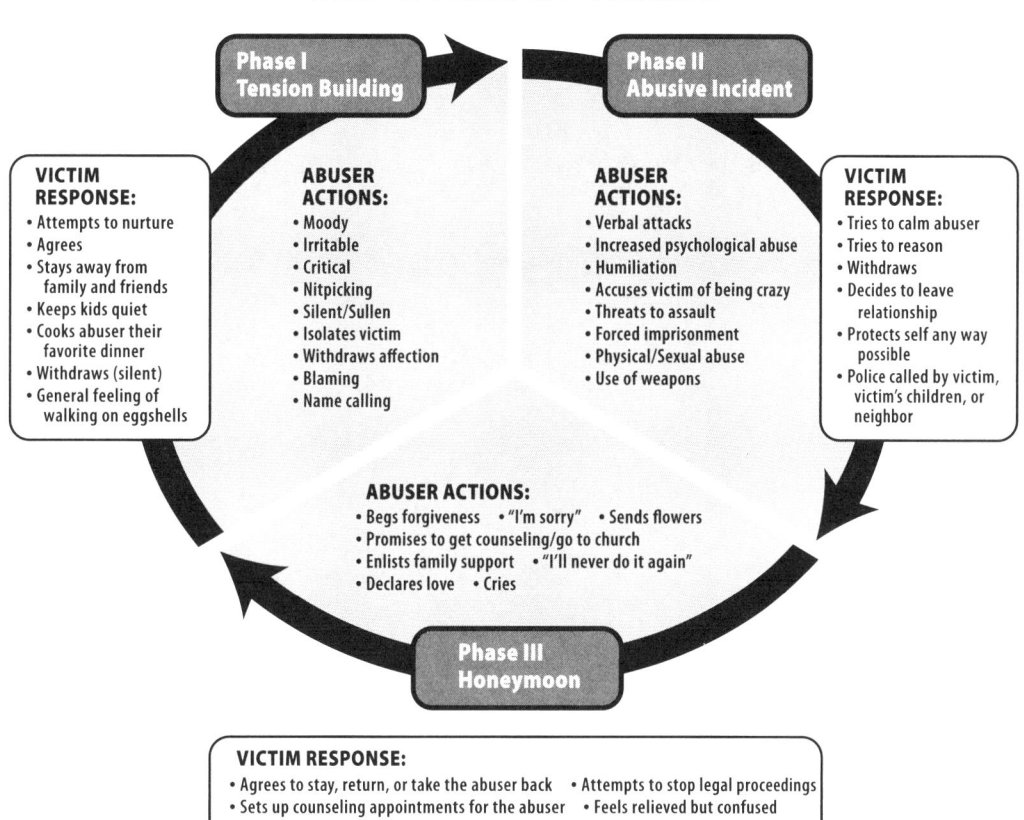

THE CYCLE OF ABUSE

❖ Handout

THE CYCLE OF ABUSE

Phase I — Tension Building

ABUSER ACTIONS:
- Moody
- Irritable
- Critical
- Nitpicking
- Silent/Sullen
- Isolates victim
- Withdraws affection
- Blaming
- Name calling

VICTIM RESPONSE:
- Attempts to nurture
- Agrees
- Stays away from family and friends
- Keeps kids quiet
- Cooks abuser their favorite dinner
- Withdraws (silent)
- General feeling of walking on eggshells

Phase II — Abusive Incident

ABUSER ACTIONS:
- Verbal attacks
- Increased psychological abuse
- Humiliation
- Accuses victim of being crazy
- Threats to assault
- Forced imprisonment
- Physical/Sexual abuse
- Use of weapons

VICTIM RESPONSE:
- Tries to calm abuser
- Tries to reason
- Withdraws
- Decides to leave relationship
- Protects self any way possible
- Police called by victim, victim's children, or neighbor

Phase III — Honeymoon

ABUSER ACTIONS:
- Begs forgiveness
- "I'm sorry"
- Sends flowers
- Promises to get counseling/go to church
- Enlists family support
- "I'll never do it again"
- Declares love
- Cries

VICTIM RESPONSE:
- Agrees to stay, return, or take the abuser back
- Sets up counseling appointments for the abuser
- Feels happy, hopeful
- Attempts to stop legal proceedings
- Feels relieved but confused

MAY NOT BE REPRODUCED WITHOUT PERMISSION

THE RED FLAGS OF ANGER

♦♦♦ **Handout**

Red flags are warnings. They tell us that we are entering an emotional state, a way of thinking, or a situation where we may feel really angry, lose control, and/or escalate. Becoming aware of these red flags helps us remain in control of ourselves and our behaviors.

Physical Red Flag Cues

What physical (in your body) cues tell you that you are getting really angry and beginning to escalate?

Red Flag Self-Talk

What kind of self-talk goes through your head when your anger is rising and you are beginning to escalate?

Red Flag Situations

What situations usually result in conflicts in which your anger rises and you begin to escalate?

THE FOUR-SQUARE TECHNIQUE

Handout

The *Four-Square Technique* is especially valuable when you are trying to decide how to act. It might be a decision of major consequence, like whether to be violent with someone, or more of an everyday decision, like how to express your disappointment or unhappiness with one of your kids.

Every decision you make involves four outcomes to consider:

SHORT TERM/SELF	LONG TERM/SELF
SHORT TERM/OTHER	**LONG TERM/OTHER**

For example, if you are tempted to get drunk at a party (but your wife often suffers when you do this), your *Four-Square* might look like this:

SHORT TERM/SELF	LONG TERM/SELF
GREAT!	**GUILTY**
SHORT TERM/OTHER	LONG TERM/OTHER
HURTFUL	**ANGRY/MISTRUSTING**

Practically everything that you are tempted to do, including getting angry or aggressive, will have a "Short Term/Self" square that is very appealing—otherwise you wouldn't be so tempted to do it. But before you act, it is very important to consider the other three squares. *Will this be a good decision for other people? Will this be a good decision for me in the long run?*

If the vote on the *Four-Square* is 3 to 1 against, or even 2 to 2, it is usually best to not go there.

HOMEWORK

Handout

It's really important to know your own RED FLAGS—so you can take corrective action before they control you.

SELF-KNOWLEDGE IS POWER.

Please rate your own RED FLAGS of anger and aggression from 1 (very mild) to 10 (extreme). Fill in the blanks wherever you see three dots (. . .).

RED FLAGS CHART

Please rate your own RED FLAGS to anger and aggression from 1 (not at all) to 10 (very). Fill in the blanks wherever you see three dots (...).

Physical RED FLAGS	1	2	3	4	5	6	7	8	9	10
1. Sweating, muscle tension or upset stomach										
2. "Pounding" sensation in head or feeling of "blood rushing"										
3. Nausea or dizziness										
4. Shaking, heart beating faster										
1. Fantasies about abusive acts										
2. Rehearsing abusive acts										
Self-talk RED FLAGS										
1. Labeling partner with words such as...										
2. I call myself a "loser" or...										
3. I tell myself she will leave me because I don't deserve her or...										
Emotional RED FLAGS										
1. Irritation, edginess										
2. Isolation, fear										
3. Jealousy										
Partner's words/actions RED FLAGS										
1. When my partner says... I am likely to become angry and aggressive										
2. When my partner does... I am likely to become angry and aggressive										

POWER & CONTROL WHEEL

◆◆◆ Handout

POWER AND CONTROL WHEEL

PHYSICAL VIOLENCE SEXUAL

USING COERCION AND THREATS
Making and/or carrying out threats to do something to hurt her • threatening to leave her, to commit suicide, to report her to welfare • making her drop charges • making her do illegal things.

USING INTIMIDATION
Making her afraid by using looks, actions, gestures • smashing things • destroying her property • abusing pets • displaying weapons.

USING ECONOMIC ABUSE
Preventing her from getting or keeping a job • making her ask for money • giving her an allowance • taking her money • not letting her know about or have access to family income.

USING EMOTIONAL ABUSE
Putting her down • making her feel bad about herself • calling her names • making her think she's crazy • playing mind games • humiliating her • making her feel guilty.

USING MALE PRIVILEGE
Treating her like a servant • making all the big decisions • acting like the "master of the castle" • being the one to define men's and women's roles

USING ISOLATION
Controlling what she does, who she sees and talks to, what she reads, where she goes • limiting her outside involvement • using jealousy to justify actions.

USING CHILDREN
Making her feel guilty about the children • using the children to relay messages • using visitation to harass her • threatening to take the children away.

MINIMIZING, DENYING AND BLAMING
Making light of the abuse and not taking her concerns about it seriously • saying the abuse didn't happen • shifting responsibility for abusive behavior • saying she caused it.

PHYSICAL VIOLENCE SEXUAL

MAY NOT BE REPRODUCED WITHOUT PERMISSION

THREATS & INTIMIDATION

◆◆◆ Handout

1. *There are multiple ways that someone in an intimate partner relationship can communicate PHYSICAL THREAT and INTIMIDATION to his or her partner:*

    VERBAL
    - *I'm going to kill you*
    - *You're never going to see your kids again*

    THREATENING BEHAVIORS
    - Getting in your partner's face
    - Hovering over your partner
    - Driving recklessly with your partner in the car

    SECRET MESSAGES
    - Sitting in the kitchen cleaning your weapon when she comes after a night out without you
    - Giving the look that victims describe this way: *All he had to do was* look *at me* ***that way*** *and I would do whatever he wanted*

    What are other ways that physical threats can get communicated?

2. There are also many kinds of threats of harming someone that do involve physical damage:

    THREATS TO EXPOSE
    - *I'm going to put those nude photos of you all over social media*
    - *If you try and leave me, your mother's going to find out about that secret abortion you had when you were a teenager*

    THREATS TO INTERFERE
    - *I'm going to make a big scene for you at work and get you fired*

    THREATS TO PROPERTY
    - *All those family photos of yours are going right into the fire!*

    THREATS OF SELF-HARM
    - *I'm going to kill myself—is that what you want?*

    What are some other threats or intimidating behaviors that aren't necessarily physical?

HOMEWORK

◆ Handout

Identify three different categories from the *Power & Control Wheel* that you have used in your relationship with your partner; include specific examples.

If you don't think this applies in your relationship, think of examples in the family you grew up in or in another relationship you know:

1. CATEGORY:

   SPECIFIC EXAMPLE:

2. CATEGORY:

   SPECIFIC EXAMPLE:

3. CATEGORY:

   SPECIFIC EXAMPLE:

MAY NOT BE REPRODUCED WITHOUT PERMISSION

BAD RAP WORKSHEET

♦♦♦ Handout

A = **Activating Event**	What happened?	Your wife tells you that she's really worried about your daughter.
B = **Belief/Story**	What did you tell yourself about this?	*Once again, she's trying to make it seem like she's a better parent than I am because she's more concerned.*
C = **Feeling/ Behavior**	What did you feel? What did you do?	Hurt/Devalued/Angry Told her: *You think you're the only one that cares???*
D = **New Belief**	What different belief is possible?	*She's really worried and wants help from me.*
E = **New Feeling/ New Behavior**	What is the new feeling and response?	Concerned/Empathetic/Valued Told her: *I know. I am too. Tell me more about what you're worried about.*

BAD RAP*

◆ Handout

1. **BLACK & WHITE:** *Seeing things as all or nothing. Beware of words like "never," "always," "nothing," and "everyone."*

    Real men don't admit their mistakes.
    You're either on my side or you're not.

2. **MINIMIZING:** *Downplaying your achievements.*

    Even though I finally made supervisor, it's no big deal.
    I did well, but so did a lot of other people.
    My counselor just gives me good feedback because she's paid to say it.

3. **MINDREADING:** *Assuming that others think something without checking it out.*

    I know my boss hates me—he gave me a dirty look.
    She's avoiding me—she must be pretty mad.
    My girlfriend didn't call me today—she must not care about me.

4. **AWFULIZING:** *Predicting that things will turn out "awful" for you.*

    My boss will never trust me again.
    I know I'm not going to make it through this place.
    Wow, he is so good at that—I'll never be able to do it that well!

5. **ERROR IN BLAMING:** *Unfairly blaming yourself—or others.*

    It's all my fault, or *It's all their fault.*
    It's my fault my son is shy.
    You always mess everything up for me.

6. **DOWN-PUTTING:** *Making too much of your mistakes (opposite of* **MINIMIZING***).*

    I failed this test; I must be dumb.
    I'm in counseling; there must be something really wrong with me.
    She doesn't like me; I must be ugly.

7. **EMOTIONAL REASONING:** *Concluding that if you feel a certain way about yourself, then it must be true.*

    Since I feel bad about myself, I must be a bad person.
    I feel rejected, so everybody must be rejecting me.
    Since I feel guilty, I must have done something wrong.

BAD RAP QUIZ*

◆ Handout

The counselor told me I'm doing better, but I know he tells that to everybody.

Ever since that red-haired girl Linda hurt me, I know redheads can't be trusted.

If I'm angry, there must be something to be angry about.

Nothing's ever going to work out for me.

It's your fault we never do anything fun.

My parents got divorced; it must have been something about me.

I sometimes don't get things right, so I must be lazy or stupid.

I feel lonely, so I guess nobody likes me.

That supervisor shows me no respect; nobody in this organization cares a damn about me.

---

*Adapted with permission from Wexler, 1991.

EXAMPLES OF ANGER-PRODUCING SELF-TALK

◆ **Handout**

She called me a name.

This proves she doesn't show me respect.

I have to protect my honor.

I will show her what it feels like by calling her a name.

I have a right to pay her back for what she has done to me.

— —

My supervisor is telling me I did something wrong.

I feel embarrassed.

He is trying to embarrass me.

If I don't stand up to him, other people will think they can take advantage of me.

People do this to me all the time, and I'm sick and tired of it.

Now is the time to prove to everyone that I must be taken seriously.

I will do whatever it takes to make sure everyone understands this!

HOMEWORK

◆◆◆ Handout

Pick out an event over the next week when you caught yourself engaging in *Bad Rap*—and turned it around—and fill out the chart below.

A = Activating Event	What happened?	
B = Belief/Story	What did you tell yourself about this?	
C = Feeling/ Behavior	What did you feel? What did you do?	
D = New Belief	What different belief is possible?	
E = New Feeling/ New Behavior	What is the new feeling and response?	

MEN ARE SUPPOSED TO . . .

♦ **Handout**

Men are supposed to be . . .

1.

2.

3.

4.

Men are supposed to do . . .

1.

2.

3.

4.

Men are supposed to have . . .

1.

2.

3.

4.

Men are *not* supposed to . . .

1.

2.

3.

4.

MASCULINITY TRAPS*

◆◆◆ Handout

As you review the self-talk that represents masculinity traps, ask yourself the following questions:

1. Which of these masculinity traps do you recognize in yourself?
2. Would you like your son to grow up with these masculinity traps? Why or why not?
3. How do men suffer when they are stuck with these masculinity traps?
4. What are some of the positive aspects of these beliefs?

I can never show my feelings. Always be tough.
- Never show any weakness.
- Never do anything "feminine."
- I have to be in control at all times.

I must win.
- I must be successful at everything!
- Don't back down from a fight.
- Always try to win arguments.
- Be on top by finding fault in others.
- Real men solve problems by force.

My possessions and success are the measure of who I am.
- My value is equal to my paycheck.
- My car and my clothes and my house prove what kind of man I am.

---

*Personal communication, Daniel G. Saunders, Ph.D., May 1999

HOMEWORK

◆ Handout

In the *It's Just a Choice* video, when the man has verbally and physically assaulted his wife, what would you have said to him after he told you what he had done?

And what would you have said to him when he complained about how "disrespectful" she was by walking away from him?

GUIDELINES FOR GOOD MEN

♦♦♦ **Handout**

1. Think of the changes that you are being called upon to make as choosing actions of "real men" and "relational heroes." Think about this in men's language, such as "taking charge," becoming powerful," and being "captain of your own ship."

2. Take personal responsibility. You are not a victim of a bad childhood, life's stresses, or a nagging girlfriend. Real men don't make excuses.

3. Learn to tolerate distress. Feeling bad is not necessarily a cause for escape, avoidance, or immediate corrective action. Real men can handle negative emotions by talking and thinking—and only then taking possible smart actions.

4. Be very careful how you describe the events in your relationships. Take responsibility for your moods. Just because you feel injured or self-doubting does not necessarily mean that your partner has *tried* to make you feel that way.

5. Even when you have done something destructive in a relationship, you are still a "good man behaving badly" or a "good man acting cluelessly." Build the good-man part while you analyze and correct the behaving-badly part.

6. Keep a running list of times when you are tempted to act badly in a relationship but instead find a different way. These can serve as nuggets of hope and models to guide you in the future.

7. Do whatever you can to let the other key people in your relationships (partners and children) know that you believe in them and appreciate what they are going through—even if you do not always like their actions.

8. Be a responsible leader and bystander. Don't laugh and implicitly approve of other men who mistreat women or children.

9. Think of your kids all the time. Act in ways that you want them to model throughout their lives.

10. Take a chance. When you sense that the woman in your life needs emotional support or needs to hear more about you, talk to her. Admit if you feel helpless or don't know what to say or do.

11. Take care of your side of the street, even when you believe that she/he/they are not taking care of hers/his/theirs.

12. Take a chance. Try talking to other men about some of your feelings. Share not just your incessant complaints but your actual fears, self-doubts, worries, etc. Tell them about things you have done or said in your relationships that you regret.

13. This may not be easy, but try learning how to validate yourself instead of depending on a woman to validate you. Or try to find other ways to get this validation that neither lead you to withdraw emotionally from your partner nor otherwise threaten your primary relationship. Remember that it is healthy to need, unhealthy to need excessively, and essential to do nothing that is fundamentally disrespectful to someone you love and need.

HOMEWORK

Handout

Review *Guidelines for Good Men*. Add one more guideline that you would want to pass on to other men:

JEALOUSY*

◆◆◆ Handout

Jealousy is one of those emotions that can tie our stomach in knots in a hurry. It is completely normal to feel a little jealous from time to time, even in the healthiest of relationships.

However, jealousy becomes a problem when you . . .

- *spend too much energy worrying about losing a loved one*
- *let jealousy build and you try to control someone else through aggression*
- *stifle a relationship by placing extreme restrictions on your partner*

Depression, anxiety, insecurity, and shame can all make someone more sensitive to perceptions of threat in their intimate partner relationship.

Pete got himself really worked up whenever he went to a party with his wife, Tania. Other men were very friendly to her, and she was very friendly and outgoing herself. Pete was afraid that she would find another man more attractive and exciting than he was. He usually picked some sort of fight with her after the party, never telling her what he was really upset about.

One day after one of these fights, Pete was thinking about how upset he made himself with jealousy. He tried to look at the situation the way an outside observer would.

After a while he was able to say to himself: *My wife is very attractive, but that doesn't mean I'm going to lose her. She hasn't given me any reason to doubt her. My fear and anger come from doubting my self-worth. If other men like her, it only confirms what I already know!*

Joe's jealousy was even stronger than Pete's. He would question his girlfriend at length when she came home, asking where she had been, who she had been with, and the details of her activities. He sometimes tore himself up wondering if she was having an affair. He would get urges to follow her everywhere or demand that she stay home. It seemed that the more he questioned her, the more he disbelieved her.

It was after hearing his friend talk about wanting to have an affair that Joe realized what was happening. The times when he was most suspicious of his girlfriend were the times when *he* was having sexual or romantic fantasies about *other women.* Now when he noticed jealousy, he asked himself: "Am I just thinking that she's having these fantasies because I'm feeling guilty about my own?"

Richard found that the best way for him to tame the jealousy monster was to let his wife know when he felt jealous. He felt very relieved being able to talk about it. Sometimes they could laugh about it together. Instead of responding with ridicule, his wife seemed to respect him more. Both of them went on to say what behavior from each other they could and could not tolerate—affairs, flirting, having friends of the opposite sex, etc. They were able to work out some contracts that specified the limits of the relationship.

What Pete, Joe, and Richard learned about taming jealousy was:

1. Some jealousy is normal, and it's best to talk about it rather than hide it.

2. You can choose to see your partner's attractiveness and behavior in the most negative possible way—or you can turn it around and see it in a way that is not such a threat.

*Thanks to Daniel G. Saunders, Ph.D., for contributing these ideas.

3. It will help to ask yourself: *Is my jealousy coming from my guilt about my own fantasies or behavior?*

4. You have the right to request and contract for some specific limits on your partner's behavior (not thoughts)—and she has the same right.

MISINTERPRETATIONS*

◆◆◆ **Handout**

Research shows that the way people think about their partner—the stories they tell themselves about the situation—plays a key role in launching abusive behavior.

The stories most likely to trigger abusive behavior are often generated by reading negative intent, or making hostile interpretations. A man who has been abusive is much more likely to think that his wife's or girlfriend's behavior was *intended* to hurt and humiliate him. This man was not able to just attribute her behavior to the fact that she is different from him or that she wasn't thinking or even that she may have been insensitive in that situation.

Discuss your self-talk *about your partner's intentions* in these situations:

You are at a barbecue and you notice that, for the past half-hour, your wife has been talking and laughing with an attractive man. He seems to be flirting with her.

You are interested in sex and let your girlfriend know this. She isn't very interested but agrees to have sex. You begin to start things, making romantic moves. After a little while, you notice that she isn't very responsive; she doesn't seem to be very turned on or interested in what you are doing.

Men who are more likely to get abusive typically have hostile interpretations of their partner:

"She was trying to make me angry."

"She was trying to put me down."

"She was trying to power trip me."

"She was trying to pick a fight."

Other men might have more neutral or even positive interpretations like these:

"I wish she would spend some more time with me here; I'll go over and talk with her."

"She sometimes forgets that I'm not a good mixer; I'll talk to her about what I need the next time we go out."

"I'm glad she's having a good time. It's a relief to me that I don't have to take care of her in social situations."

"I'm kind of disappointed, but there are plenty of reasons why she doesn't want to have sex right now—no big deal."

---

*Adapted with permission from Holtzworth-Munroe & Hutchinson, 1993.

HOMEWORK

Handout

1. Record three situations in which you experience jealousy over the next week. These can include anything from strong feelings (like seeing your wife or partner flirting with another man) to mild feelings (like observing your supervisor give approval to someone else). If you do not notice any jealousy this week, recall experiences from previous weeks.

   a.

   b.

   c.

NORMATIVE MALE ALEXITHYMIA

♦♦♦ **Handout**

Normative Male Alexithymia is a technical term for the way many men have trouble figuring out what they are really feeling and finding a way to express this information to others. Alexithymia is a word with Greek origins that means "without words for feelings."

Which of these do you recognize in yourself?

- *I am often confused about which emotion I am feeling.*
- *It is easy for me to find the right words for my feelings.*
- *When I am upset, I don't know if I am sad, frightened, or angry.*
- *I am often puzzled by sensations in my body.*
- *People tell me to describe my feelings in more detail.*

Below is a list of some of the more common feelings. The only way most of us (particularly men) learn how to label our different feelings is by being around other people who give us some feedback.

For example, when you were a baby, you didn't know the names of the different colors. Someone kept telling you that the sky was blue and that the fire engine was red. You learned, after more experiences, that red has many different shades: scarlet is different from pink, and maroon is not quite the same as burgundy.

The same is true for feelings.

- *Excited*
- *Tender*
- *Sad*
- *Lonely*
- *Edgy*
- *Frustrated*
- *Frightened*
- *Contented*

- *Depressed*
- *Timid*
- *Hurt*
- *Jealous*
- *Loving*
- *Elated*
- *Happy*

ANGER IS A SECONDARY EMOTION

◆ Handout

Many people (especially men) are very comfortable identifying and expressing being "pissed off." It feels safe. It feels powerful. It does not feel vulnerable. And being pissed off is certainly appropriate in many situations.

However . . . **ANGER IS A *SECONDARY* EMOTION**. It is almost always preceded by a primary emotion that feels like a wound, attack, or anxiety.

It is extremely valuable for all of us to have the ability to label our emotions properly. Think of a recent time when you felt angry, then identify the specific painful feeling you were experiencing that probably triggered it. This is the *core hurt*. Here are some examples:

- *I felt disrespected.*
- *I felt confused and unsure.*
- *I felt unimportant.*
- *I felt rejected.*
- *I felt unlovable.*
- *I felt powerless.*
- *I felt ignored.*

We are not telling you that anger is not real. It is very real. It's just not the whole story.

In the future, whenever you notice anger, ask yourself this question: *What is my underlying feeling and core hurt?* If you are able to do this, you will be in a much more powerful position to truly run your own emotional and behavioral life. You will no longer be controlled by your anger.

HOMEWORK

◆◆◆ Handout

1. Over the next week, pay attention to your feelings. Record at least one example from each category of feelings:

   Sadness—What was the Situation?

   Self-Talk:

   Description of Feeling:

   Joy—What was the Situation?

   Self-Talk:

   Description of Feeling:

   Fear (Anxiety)—What was the Situation?

   Self-Talk:

   Description of Feeling:

   Anger—What was the Situation?

   Self-Talk:

   Description of Feeling:

SWITCH!

◆◆◆ Handout

1. ***What went wrong?***

   Describe a time, that you now deeply regret, when you became aggressive to your partner or children.

2. ***What was my self-talk?***

   What was your self-talk before the build-up to this that led you to lose it like that?

3. ***What new, more productive self-talk could I have used?***

   What would you like to have said to yourself instead in this situation that would have led you down a different path?

4. ***The group yells "Switch."***

   Put yourself back in the problem situation. Practice the old self-talk out loud and get yourself back into the scene. When the group yells **"Switch!"** switch over to your productive self-talk instead.

5. ***What do you think? What does the group think?***

   Do you think this would have led to a different outcome? And . . . do you REALLY think you could use this new self-talk in the future? What might get in your way?

HOMEWORK

◆◆◆ Handout

If you did not get a chance to do the *Switch!* exercise in the group, fill out your own below. And if you did the exercise in the group, pick another incident and go through the same steps. Pick a time in your relationship when you reacted in a way that you now regret.

SITUATION AND YOUR REACTION:

OLD SELF-TALK:

NEW SELF-TALK:

PREDICTED NEW REACTION:

PUT-DOWNS FROM PARENTS*

◆ **Handout**

Please write in the number below (1–4) that best describes how often the experience happened to you with your mother (or stepmother, female guardian, etc.) and father (or stepfather, male guardian, etc.) when you were growing up. If you had more than one mother/father figure, please answer based on the person whom you feel played the most significant role in your upbringing.

You may choose to share your responses with the group, but that decision will be *completely* up to you. The more honest you can be as you describe yourself and your history, the more you will be able to benefit from this program.

1	2	3	4
Never occurred	Occasionally Occurred	Sometimes Occurred	Frequently Occurred

Mother　　　　　　　　　　　　　　　　　　　　　　　　　　　　　　Father

1. I think that my parent wished I had been a really different kind of child. _____ _____
2. As a child, I was physically punished or scolded in the presence of others. _____ _____
3. I was treated as the "scapegoat" of the family. _____ _____
4. I felt my parent thought it was my fault when he/she was unhappy. _____ _____
5. I think my parent was mean and held grudges towards me _____ _____
6. I was punished by my parents without having done anything. _____ _____
7. My parent criticized me and/or told me how useless I was in front of others. _____ _____
8. My parent beat me for no reason. _____ _____
9. My parent would be angry with me without letting me know why. _____ _____

---

*Adapted with permission from Dutton, van Ginkel, & Strazomski (1995) from the *EMBU: Memories of My Upbringing* scale.

MAY NOT BE REPRODUCED WITHOUT PERMISSION

HOMEWORK*

◆◆◆ **Handout**

Fill out the *Put-Downs from Parents* chart again, this time from the perspective of one of your own children. If you do not have children, pick a child you know well and try to fill it out from his or her perspective.

1	2	3	4
Never occurred	Occasionally Occurred	Sometimes Occurred	Frequently Occurred

                                                                               Father

Mother

1. I think that my parent wished I had been a really different kind of child. _____ _____
2. As a child, I was physically punished or scolded in the presence of others. _____ _____
3. I was treated as the "scapegoat" of the family. _____ _____
4. I felt my parent thought it was my fault when he/she was unhappy. _____ _____
5. I think my parent was mean and held grudges towards me _____ _____
6. I was punished by my parents without having done anything. _____ _____
7. My parent criticized me and/or told me how useless I was in front of others. _____ _____
8. My parent beat me for no reason. _____ _____
9. My parent would be angry with me without letting me know why. _____ _____

---

*Adapted with permission from Dutton, van Ginkel, & Strazomski (1995) from the *EMBU: Memories of My Upbringing scale*.

THE MALE SHAME MANIFESTO

◆ Handout

So many of us dread shame and go to great lengths to avoid it, run from it, or defend against it—even without realizing that we are doing this. Even in intimate relationships—which are *supposed* to be safe and secure—we often make unconscious decisions about how to operate, with one or more "soundtracks" blasting beneath the surface.

Below are examples of what many men are secretly thinking. These thoughts especially get in the way of intimate partner relationships. See which of them you recognize in yourself.

- *I will do anything to avoid feeling shame.*
- *I will hide from myself.*
- *I will hide from you.*
- *I will anticipate potentially shaming experiences and avoid them.*
- *I will go on the offensive if I fear the possibility of looking bad or feeling shamed.*
- *I will numb myself if I feel shame.*
- *If I show you my real self, I risk feeling shamed (and then you will reject me).*

Discuss these with the group. Think of times when you reacted with defensiveness, aggression, withdrawal, or hostility with your partner—and see if you can identify whether any of these "soundtracks" were playing.

HOMEWORK

◆◆◆ **Handout**

Identify one time when you felt shamed with your wife or girlfriend and describe how you handled it.

THE BROKEN MIRROR SEQUENCE*

Handout

Each of us looks for a response from the people most important to us. Based on their responses, we might feel good about ourselves or just the opposite. It's like the other person is a mirror: you look into her eyes, hear her words, watch her body language, and it's either like a GOOD mirror—reflecting back a picture of yourself as somebody who is decent and lovable—or a BROKEN mirror—reflecting an image of someone who is a loser. It is completely normal and human to feel this way—it happens every day to all of us.

Some people see *broken mirrors* all over the place. If your wife says she needs to work more shifts because the family needs more money, her words might be a *broken mirror* to you: what you see is that you are not a good enough provider!

Once you see (or think that you see!) the *broken mirror*, a destructive sequence often follows. The sequence goes like this:

> EVENT: Something happens in your life.
>
> BROKEN MIRROR: You interpret it as negative and as a statement that there is something wrong with you.
>
> BAD FEELINGS: You feel bad—but you don't have the words or language to describe your feelings very well.
>
> EMOTIONAL FLOODING: The bad feelings "flood" you.
>
> TAKING ACTION: You feel the need to DO SOMETHING to make the bad feelings go away: either escape/withdraw or retaliate against the person who (in your mind) is responsible for making you feel bad.

According to this model, when you experience unbearable feelings—like hurt, shame, helplessness, fear, guilt, inadequacy, and loneliness—you frequently feel overwhelmed. So, you need to defend yourself against these feelings, although these defenses do not provide much of a solution:

- Denying responsibility and placing the blame on her: *Why do you make me feel so bad about myself?*
- Controlling everything and everyone in the vicinity: *I want you all to get out of your rooms and clean up this house now—or else!*
- Using alcohol or drugs to temporarily take away the pain
- Seeking excitement to distract from the bad feelings: *I'm going to go get laid by someone who really knows how to make a man feel good!*
- When these defenses provide relief, they are reinforced, and you learn to keep using them. But, in the long run, we all need to find a way to tolerate a wider range of negative emotions without acting out.
- Again: **If you know what you are thinking and feeling, you are in a much more powerful position to truly be in charge of your own life.**

---

*Wexler, 2004

RELATIONAL HEROISM*

◆ Handout

Every day, people are heroes—not just in the obvious ways of fighting tough wars or rescuing burning bodies from the World Trade Center or making tough decisions in the workplace, but also by the ways they behave in their relationships.

We call these acts of *Relational Heroism*. Think of it this way: in a combat zone, we call people heroic when they act in a way that puts themselves at risk or make a very tough decision for the greater good.

So, when you decide to put aside your own needs or hurt feelings in your relationship or with your kids for the greater good, you are being a hero. A *relational hero*. And if you do this over and over, you get into the *Relational Hero Hall of Fame*.

Preston was in the midst of a very rocky period in his marriage and the future was very much in doubt. He began talking to his wife about a vacation he was hoping they could go on that was almost a year away. She looked at him and said, half-joking and half-serious, *Well, you're assuming a lot, aren't you?*

Preston remembers reacting this way: *Sharice made that crack about "Well, you're assuming a lot, aren't you?" and I just shut down, like I always do. I just felt so hurt. Same old stuff. But it didn't take me long before I turned to her and told her that her comment had really hurt me, and I asked her, sort of nicely, why she had said it. And we actually had a conversation about the whole thing.*

I guess that's sort of the "relational hero" thing we've been talking about, isn't it? I guess I'm doing pretty well.

In the novel (and adapted movie) *High Fidelity,* the main character, Rob, has a long history of failed relationships and a long history of selfish behaviors that contribute to these failures. He was very skilled at putting together mix tapes of carefully selected songs for a woman he is interested in—but he would only pick songs based on what he thought she *should* be listening to. He was never able to see any woman as she really was, only as he wanted her to be.

Finally, after more and more errors and grief, he matures and has a breakthrough. He makes a mix tape for the new love of his life, Laura, which he describes like this:

> *. . . and I start to compile in my head a compilation tape for her, something that's full of stuff she's heard of, and full of stuff she'd play. Tonight, for the first time ever, I can sort of see how it's done.* (p. 323)

The task is so simple, yet it took him years to prepare for. That's *relational heroism*. It's not bold and dramatic to the outside observer, but it means so much.

---

*Real, 1997

HOMEWORK

Handout

Identify three examples of your own *relational heroism* over the next week—times when you put aside your own needs or your first, instinctive reaction and found a better way. Note the situation and how it made you feel bad about yourself. If you can't find three from this week, use examples from your past. We all have plenty of them.

1.

2.

3.

ADVERSE CHILDHOOD EXPERIENCES (ACE) INFO

Handout

- *Adverse Childhood Experiences (ACE) are very common*
- *ACE are strong predictors of later health risks*

This combination makes the ACE score one of the leading predictors of adult health and social well-being.

1. The original ACE study was conducted on 17,337 participants recruited from the Kaiser Permanente health care system between 1995 and 1997.

2. About 67% of individuals reported at least one ACE. If someone had one ACE point, they usually had more: 87% who reported one ACE reported at least one other ACE.

3. The number of childhood ACE's was strongly correlated with adult problems with:
   - *Smoking*
   - *Alcohol and drug abuse*
   - *Sexual promiscuity*
   - *Severe obesity*
   - *Depression*
   - *Heart disease*
   - *Cancer*
   - *Chronic lung disease*
   - *Shortened lifespan*
   - *Domestic violence*

4. Compared to an ACE score of zero, having four ACE points is associated with a seven-fold increase in alcoholism, a doubling of one's risk of being diagnosed with cancer, and a four-fold increase in emphysema.

ACE Score and the Risk of *Perpetrating* Domestic Violence

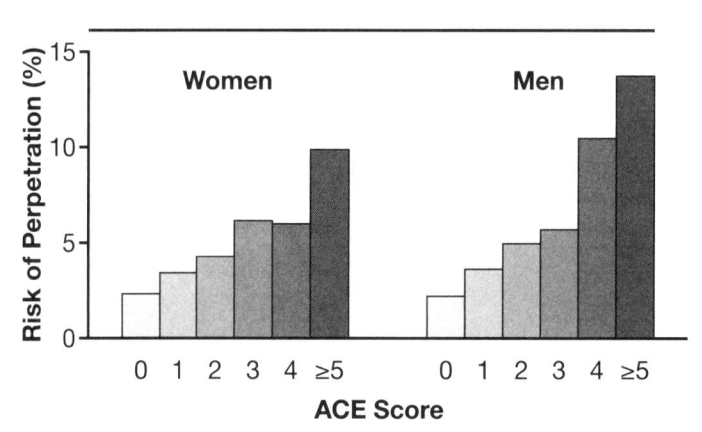

MAY NOT BE REPRODUCED WITHOUT PERMISSION

WHAT'S MY ACE SCORE?*

◆◆◆ **Handout**

Prior to your 18th birthday:

1. Did a parent or other adult in the household often or very often . . .
   Swear at you, insult you, put you down, or humiliate you?
   or
   Act in a way that made you afraid that you might be physically hurt?
                                               Yes   No   If yes enter 1 _____

2. Did a parent or other adult in the household often or very often . . .
   Push, grab, slap, or throw something at you?
   or
   Ever hit you so hard that you had marks or were injured?
                                               Yes   No   If yes enter 1 _____

3. Did an adult or person at least five years older than you ever . . .
   Touch or fondle you or have you touch their body in a sexual way?
   or
   Attempt or actually have oral, anal, or vaginal intercourse with you?
                                               Yes   No   If yes enter 1 _____

4. Did you often or very often feel that . . .
   No one in your family loved you or thought you were important or special?
   or
   Your family didn't look out for each other, feel close to each other,
   or support each other?
                                               Yes   No   If yes enter 1 _____

5. Did you often or very often feel that . . .
   You didn't have enough to eat, had to wear dirty clothes, and had
   no one to protect you?
   or
   Your parents were too drunk or high to take care of you or take you
   to the doctor if you needed it?
                                               Yes   No   If yes enter 1 _____

6. Were your parents ever separated or divorced?
                                               Yes   No   If yes enter 1 _____

---

*Felitti et al., 1998

MAY NOT BE REPRODUCED WITHOUT PERMISSION

7. Was your mother or stepmother (or father or stepfather) . . .
   Often or very often pushed, grabbed, slapped, or had something thrown at her (or him)?
   or
   Sometimes, often, or very often kicked, bitten, hit with a fist, or hit with something hard?
   or
   Ever repeatedly hit over at least a few minutes or threatened with a gun or knife?
               Yes No   If yes enter 1 _____

8. Did you live with anyone who was a problem drinker or alcoholic or who used street drugs?
               Yes No   If yes enter 1 _____

9. Was a household member depressed or mentally ill, or did a household member attempt suicide?
               Yes No   If yes enter 1 _____

10. Did a household member go to prison?
                Yes No   If yes enter 1 _____

Now add up your "Yes" answers: _____ This is your ACE Score

ACE RESILIENCE QUESTIONNAIRE

♦♦♦ **Handout**

Many childhood experiences have been found to help cushion the impact of ACE scores. These usually help protect most people with four or more ACEs from developing negative outcomes.

1. I believe that my mother loved me when I was little.
   Definitely true   Prob true   Not sure   Prob Not True   Def Not True

2. I believe that my father loved me when I was little.
   Definitely true   Prob true   Not sure   Prob Not True   Def Not True

3. When I was little, other people helped my mother and father take care of me and they seemed to love me.
   Definitely true   Prob true   Not sure   Prob Not True   Def Not True

4. I've heard that when I was an infant, someone in my family enjoyed playing with me and I enjoyed it, too.
   Definitely true   Prob true   Not sure   Prob Not True   Def Not True

5. When I was a child, there were relatives in my family who made me feel better if I was sad or worried.
   Definitely true   Prob true   Not sure   Prob Not True   Def Not True

6. When I was a child, neighbors or my friends' parents seemed to like me.
   Definitely true   Prob true   Not sure   Prob Not True   Def Not True

7. When I was a child, teachers, coaches, youth leaders, or ministers were there to help me.
   Definitely true   Prob true   Not sure   Prob Not True   Def Not True

8. Someone in my family cared about how I was doing in school.
   Definitely true   Prob true   Not sure   Prob Not True   Def Not True

9. My family, neighbors, and friends talked often about making our lives better.
   Definitely true   Prob true   Not sure   Prob Not True   Def Not True

10. We had rules in our house and were expected to follow them.
    Definitely true   Prob true   Not sure   Prob Not True   Def Not True

11. When I felt really bad, I could almost always find someone I trusted to talk to.
    Definitely true   Prob true   Not sure   Prob Not True   Def Not True

12. As a youth, people noticed that I was capable and could get things done.
    Definitely true   Prob true   Not sure   Prob Not True   Def Not True

13. I was independent and a go-getter.
   Definitely true   Prob true   Not sure   Prob Not True   Def Not True

14. I believed that life is what you make it.
   Definitely true   Prob true   Not sure   Prob Not True   Def Not True

How many of these 14 protective factors did I have as a child and youth? (How many of the 14 answers circled were "Definitely True" or "Probably True"?) _____

HOMEWORK

Handout

Fill out the *What's My ACE Score?* questionnaire again, this time from the perspective of one of your own children. If you do not have children, pick a child you know well and try to fill it out from his or her perspective.

Then do the same with the *ACE Resilience Questionnaire*, again from the child's perspective.

What's My ACE Score?

Prior to your 18th birthday:

1. Did a parent or other adult in the household often or very often . . .
   Swear at you, insult you, put you down, or humiliate you?
   or
   Act in a way that made you afraid that you might be physically hurt?
            Yes   No   If yes enter 1 _____

2. Did a parent or other adult in the household often or very often . . .
   Push, grab, slap, or throw something at you?
   or
   Ever hit you so hard that you had marks or were injured?
            Yes   No   If yes enter 1 _____

3. Did an adult or person at least five years older than you ever . . .
   Touch or fondle you or have you touch their body in a sexual way?
   or
   Attempt or actually have oral, anal, or vaginal intercourse with you?
            Yes   No   If yes enter 1 _____

4. Did you often or very often feel that . . .
   No one in your family loved you or thought you were important or special?
   or
   Your family didn't look out for each other, feel close to each other, or support each other?
            Yes   No   If yes enter 1 _____

5. Did you often or very often feel that . . .
   You didn't have enough to eat, had to wear dirty clothes, and had no one to protect you?
   or
   Your parents were too drunk or high to take care of you or take you to the doctor if you needed it?
            Yes   No   If yes enter 1 _____

6. Were your parents ever separated or divorced?
            Yes   No   If yes enter 1 _____

MAY NOT BE REPRODUCED WITHOUT PERMISSION

7. Was your mother or stepmother (or father or stepfather) . . .
   Often or very often pushed, grabbed, slapped, or had something thrown at her (or him)?
   or
   Sometimes, often, or very often kicked, bitten, hit with a fist, or hit with something hard?
   or
   Ever repeatedly hit over at least a few minutes or threatened with a gun or knife?

   Yes   No   If yes enter 1 _____

8. Did you live with anyone who was a problem drinker or alcoholic or who used street drugs?

   Yes   No   If yes enter 1 _____

9. Was a household member depressed or mentally ill, or did a household member attempt suicide?

   Yes   No   If yes enter 1 _____

10. Did a household member go to prison?

    Yes   No   If yes enter 1 _____

Now add up your "Yes" answers: _____ This is your ACE Score

ACE RESILIENCE Questionnaire

Many childhood experiences have been found to help cushion the impact of ACE scores. These usually help protect most people with four or more ACEs from developing negative outcomes.

1. I believe that my mother loved me when I was little.
   Definitely true   Prob true   Not sure   Prob Not True   Def Not True

2. I believe that my father loved me when I was little.
   Definitely true   Prob true   Not sure   Prob Not True   Def Not True

3. When I was little, other people helped my mother and father take care of me and they seemed to love me.
   Definitely true   Prob true   Not sure   Prob Not True   Def Not True

4. I've heard that when I was an infant, someone in my family enjoyed playing with me and I enjoyed it, too.
   Definitely true   Prob true   Not sure   Prob Not True   Def Not True

5. When I was a child, there were relatives in my family who made me feel better if I was sad or worried.
   Definitely true   Prob true   Not sure   Prob Not True   Def Not True

6. When I was a child, neighbors or my friends' parents seemed to like me.
   Definitely true   Prob true   Not sure   Prob Not True   Def Not True

MAY NOT BE REPRODUCED WITHOUT PERMISSION

7. When I was a child, teachers, coaches, youth leaders, or ministers were there to help me.
   Definitely true   Prob true   Not sure   Prob Not True   Def Not True

8. Someone in my family cared about how I was doing in school.
   Definitely true   Prob true   Not sure   Prob Not True   Def Not True

9. My family, neighbors, and friends talked often about making our lives better.
   Definitely true   Prob true   Not sure   Prob Not True   Def Not True

10. We had rules in our house and were expected to follow them.
    Definitely true   Prob true   Not sure   Prob Not True   Def Not True

11. When I felt really bad, I could almost always find someone I trusted to talk to.
    Definitely true   Prob true   Not sure   Prob Not True   Def Not True

12. As a youth, people noticed that I was capable and could get things done.
    Definitely true   Prob true   Not sure   Prob Not True   Def Not True

13. I was independent and a go-getter.
    Definitely true   Prob true   Not sure   Prob Not True   Def Not True

14. I believed that life is what you make it.
    Definitely true   Prob true   Not sure   Prob Not True   Def Not True

How many of these 14 protective factors did I have as a child and youth? (How many of the 14 answers circled were "Definitely True" or "Probably True"?) _____

ASSERTIVENESS

♦♦♦ **Handout**

ASSERTIVENESS: TAKING CARE OF YOUR OWN NEEDS, THOUGHTS, AND FEELINGS IN A WAY THAT IS LEAST LIKELY TO MAKE THE OTHER PERSON FEEL ATTACKED OR ACT DEFENSIVE

ASSERTIVE: This behavior involves knowing what you feel and want. It also involves expressing your feelings and needs directly and honestly without violating the rights of others. You are accepting responsibility for your feelings and actions:

It bothered me when you were late coming back from shopping because I had to rush off to work.

AGGRESSIVE: You attack someone else, get controlling, provoking, and maybe even violent. Its consequences could be destructive to others as well as yourself.

What the hell's wrong with you? All you ever think about is yourself!

PASSIVE: You withdraw, becomes anxious, and avoid confrontation. Passive people let others think for them, make decisions for them, and tell them what to do.

You feel resentful but you don't express it or deal with it. You feel like it's useless: either you don't deserve any better, or it's just hopeless. You may get depressed, and you may believe that your wife or partner is purposely trying to take advantage of you—but you don't do anything about the situation.

PASSIVE-AGGRESSIVE: In this behavior you are not direct in relating to people and you don't accept what is happening—but you retaliate in an indirect manner. This type of behavior can cause confusion. The other person feels "stung" but can't be exactly sure how or why. And you can act like you've done nothing at all—and imply that your partner is just "too sensitive."

You act cold to your girlfriend, then pretend like nothing's wrong when she asks you about it.

Or you're feeling unappreciated by your wife and you "forget" to give her a phone message. Or you make some "joking" comment about her weight.

PASSIVE-ASSERTIVE: There are plenty of situations when you may "assertively" choose to be "passive." And this is often a GOOD choice. When your partner is in a bad mood and complaining about things that are not really fair, sometimes—in the most successful of relationships—you might just choose to let it go. Doing this sometimes can be very positive for you and for the relationship. The same is true when an employee chooses to keep his mouth shut even when he doesn't like an office policy (thanks to Genevieve Olucha, Ph.D., for this concept).

MAY NOT BE REPRODUCED WITHOUT PERMISSION

WHAT IS ASSERTIVE BEHAVIOR?

Handout

1. Asking for what you want but not being demanding.
2. Expressing feelings.
3. Genuinely expressing feedback or compliments to others and accepting them.
4. Disagreeing, without being aggressive.
5. Asking questions and getting information from others.
6. Using "I" messages and "I feel" statements without being judgmental or blaming.
7. Making eye contact during a conversation (unless this is inappropriate in the person's culture).

EXAMPLES:

- *Can you give me some feedback about how I handled the kids' homework tonight?*
- *I feel embarrassed when you tease me about my weight in front of my friends.*
- *Mom, I know you want us to call more often, but I don't think you realize how busy we both are.*
- *Corey, I just saw your report card and I'm concerned. Let's sit down and talk about this together.*
- *Sarah, I'd like to talk about this later after we've both cooled off.*
- *I really care about you; let's work this out.*

ASKING FOR CHANGE

Handout

This is a communication technique for when you would like the other person to change something. The goal (as with all assertive communication) is to **communicate clearly and respectfully in a way that is least likely to put the other person on the defensive**. Why? Because it works.

Construct "I" messages by using these phrases:

WHEN YOU . . . (just describe, don't blame)

I FEEL . . . (state the feeling) because . . . (explain in more detail)

Note: Using the word because with an explanation can help by giving the other person more information to understand you.

I WISH . . . /I WOULD APPRECIATE IF . . . (specify new behavior you want the other person to use instead)

AND IF YOU CAN DO THAT, I WILL . . . (explain how the other person will benefit)

The different parts of the "I" message do not have to be delivered in this exact order. The important thing is to keep the focus on yourself and to stay away from blame.

- *When you take long phone calls during dinner,*
- *I feel angry because I begin to think you don't want to talk to me.*
- *I wish you would tell whoever's calling that you'll call them back because we're in the middle of dinner.*
- *And if you can do that, I'll make sure not to hassle you about being on the phone later.*

- *When you don't come home when you said you would,*
- *I get worried that something has happened to you.*
- *I would really like you to text me if you're going to be late.*
- *And if you can do that, I promise not to have an attitude when you get home.*

- *When you demand something from me right in the middle of a busy time at work,*
- *I get so rattled that I end up making more mistakes.*
- *I wish that you would lighten up when you know that I'm busy.*
- *And if you can do that, I will be a lot easier to work with.*

MAY NOT BE REPRODUCED WITHOUT PERMISSION

CLASSIC MISTAKES:

- Being too vague: *When you are selfish . . .*

- Putting down their character (*You are so controlling!*) instead of describing a specific behavior (*Last night it bothered me that you gave me so many instructions about the kids*).

- Saying *I feel that you* (judgment) . . . instead of *I feel* (emotion).

- Not offering a specific and realistic new behavior (like if you ask someone to change a key and unchangeable part of their personality: *I want you to become a more outgoing person*).

- Feeling like you need to reward the other person with something specific, like a back rub or cleaning out the garage. Sometimes that's appropriate, but many times a reward of *I'll feel better and it will help our relationship* is plenty.

HOMEWORK

Handout

Practice the *ASKING FOR CHANGE* model with your partner or somebody else close to you. It's usually a good idea to explain in advance that you are trying out something new and that you would like their feedback on how it works. Record the four steps you tried and be prepared to discuss in group:

WHEN YOU . . .

I FEEL . . .

I WISH . . . (or I WOULD APPRECIATE IF . . .)

AND IF YOU CAN DO THAT, I WILL . . .

EXPRESSING YOUR FEELINGS

♦ Handout

For each situation below . . .

- Identify your feelings.
- Put into words how you might express your feelings. Remember to use "I feel" statements.
- Remember that you don't always have to respond. If you would choose to say nothing in any of these situations, describe your feelings.

1. Your girlfriend was going to meet you downtown for lunch, and you have been waiting for over an hour. She finally arrives and says she had a few errands to run before she came.

2. A friend of yours makes a "joking" comment about how your wife has "really put on some weight lately."

3. Your wife teases you in front of your friends about how much trouble you have trying to fix things around the house.

4. You are late getting home and your wife or partner demands an explanation, but as soon as you begin she interrupts and starts yelling and saying how inconsiderate you are.

ACTIVE LISTENING

Handout

Active listening is a communication technique that encourages the other person to continue speaking. It also enables you to be certain you understand what the other person is saying. It's a way of checking it out. It's called active listening because you not only listen but also actively let the other person know that you have really heard her.

A. Active listening involves PARAPHRASING.

Paraphrasing is stating in your own words what you think the other person has said.

- *You sound really (feeling) about (situation).*
- *You must really feel . . . (state a feeling).*
- *What I hear you saying is _____.*

B. Active listening also involves CLARIFYING.

Clarifying involves asking questions to get more information.
Clarifying helps you hear more specifics about the situation and feelings.
Clarifying also lets the other person know you are interested in what he or she is saying.

- *So tell me what happened that got you so upset.*
- *How did you feel when that happened?*

C. Active listening often involves PERSONALIZING.

Personalizing involves offering a personal example of feeling the same thing or being in the same situation.

- *I think I know what you mean. I've been there too.*
- *I felt the same way when I lost my job. I think everyone does.*

Personalizing helps the other person feel less alone, and it implies that someone else has experienced this and has recovered from it.

Personalizing can be harmful if you talk too much about yourself and steal the spotlight from the person who needs it.

- *You think that was bad? Listen to what happened to me!*

D. Active listening does *not* mean cheering someone up, defending yourself, judging the person, or just repeating back exactly what was said.

All I ever do is the dirty work around here!

- *Oh, come on, it's a hot day, you're just in a bad mood, don't worry about it.*

You can't trust anyone around this place!

- *Now, now, it's okay. It's all going to be better—I'll take care of it for you.*

I'm really worried that my family is going to be mad at me for dropping out of school.

- *You shouldn't feel that way.*

I keep trying to talk to you about how to handle the kids and you never listen to me!

- *I'm in charge! No more discussion!*

This place is really disgusting.

- *It sounds like you think this place is really disgusting.*

Some keys to being a GOOD ACTIVE LISTENER:

- Good eye contact, leaning slightly forward, reinforcing by nodding or paraphrasing
- Clarifying by asking questions
- Avoiding distractions
- Trying to really understand what the other person is really saying

HOMEWORK #1

Handout

Record three examples of your active listening responses over the next week.

Situation:

You said:

- -

Situation:

You said:

- -

Situation:

You said:

HOMEWORK #2

Handout

NOTE: This homework exercise must be completed online—see instructions below.

1. Go the web page at
   https://www.5lovelanguages.com/profile/couples/

2. Fill out the information to get started on the quiz.

3. Complete this quiz online (should take 5-10 minutes).

4. Print results indicating your *Love Languages Personal Profile* and bring it with you to the next group session.

MAY NOT BE REPRODUCED WITHOUT PERMISSION

THE FIVE LOVE LANGUAGES

Handout

(based on ideas from Chapman, G. [2010]. *The 5 Love Languages: The Secret to Love That Lasts*. Chicago: Northfield Publishing)

1. If you really love someone, you find a way to love that person the way she really wants to be loved.

2. Sometimes (often!) love languages are mismatched. This does not have to be a major problem—as long as you recognize your partner's language and try to speak to her in that language. And, when you feel like you are not being loved, remember that your partner may be showing love in a different language.

3. As you think about these love languages, remember that you are identifying what is most important to you. You are NOT evaluating your partner's performance.

PHYSICAL TOUCH

This is not just about sex. It's about the thousand little forms of physical affection that loving couples offer each other every day of the week. For a person whose primary language is *Physical Touch*, hugs, hand-holding, and cuddling in bed together are the most powerful ways to show excitement, concern, care, and love. It feeds the person's sense of security in this relationship.

QUALITY TIME

Undivided attention means everything for the person whose primary love language is *Quality Time*. This can range from something dramatic like a weekend away, or a walk on the beach, or even just going to the supermarket together. Sometimes it means a very meaningful conversation, but not always. The attention is especially meaningful if there are no distractions—no texting, no screen time, no distractions.

WORDS OF AFFIRMATION

Actions don't always speak louder than words. If this is a person's love language, unsolicited compliments are worth more than a diamond necklace or explosive sex. Hearing the words, "I love you," or "I really appreciate you" or "Everything with you is fun" can fill and sustain the person at a very deep level. In contrast: insults can leave the person shattered and are not easily forgotten.

ACTS OF SERVICE

Folding laundry, picking something up from the store, making a phone call that the other person dreads making—these can all ease the burden of responsibilities weighing on the partner. If you don't follow through or actually create more work for your partner, you are communicating that your partner's feelings don't matter. Helping out with tasks that are stressful or a burden to this person is the best way to convey your love and want to be there to help.

RECEIVING GIFTS

This is not just about materialism. If this is a primary love language, the gifts represent that the giver is thinking about his or her partner and puts care and effort into making the partner happy. It can be something as big as expensive jewelry or something as small as the partner's favorite chocolate chip cookie. The gift also serves as an ongoing physical reminder of the love.

HOMEWORK*

◆◆◆ Handout

COMMUNICATION ROADBLOCKS—THE "ANTI-LOVE" LANGUAGES

We often block communication by using these kinds of responses. Check any of the following that you have ever used with your partner. Write in a personal example for at least three categories.

1. ____ ORDERING/DIRECTING/COMMANDING

   Don't talk about your mother like that.
   Stop complaining.

2. ____ WARNING/THREATENING

   If you do that, you'll be sorry.
   I can dish it out too, you know!

3. ____ MORALIZING/PREACHING/SHOULDS

   You shouldn't act like that.
   A real man would never treat a woman like that.

4. ____ ADVISING/GIVING SOLUTIONS

   If you don't like it, you should just leave.

5. ____ JUDGING/CRITICIZING/NAME-CALLING/LABELING

   You are so stupid that you never get anything right!
   You will always be a loser.

6. ____ REASSURING/SYMPATHIZING/CONSOLING

   You'll feel different tomorrow.
   Just forget it; it's no big deal.

7. ____ INTERPRETING/ANALYZING/DIAGNOSING

   This is because of your unresolved issues with your father.

8. ____ SARCASM/HUMOR

   Oh, you're going to start crying now???

---

*Adapted from Larance, L. Y., Hoffman-Ruzicka, A., & Shivas, J. B. (2009)

HOMEWORK

◆◆◆ Handout

Write one paragraph (at least 100 words) as if you are your wife or partner. The subject is "Sometimes I don't trust my husband (or partner) because . . ."

FOUR HORSEMEN OF THE APOCALYPSE

♦♦♦ **Handout**

ACCUSATIONS (CRITICISM): Complaints are expressed in a destructive manner, as an attack on the other person's character: You're so thoughtless and self-centered!

In a constructive complaint, the person states specifically what is upsetting her, and constructively criticizes the other person's action, not the person himself, saying how it made her feel.

CONTEMPT (DISGUST): Contempt is usually expressed not just in the words themselves but also in a tone of voice and an angry expression. Rolling the eyes. A look of disgust.

What distinguishes contempt is the intention to insult and psychologically abuse the other person. When contempt begins to overwhelm the relationship, one person tends to forget, entirely, the other person's positive qualities, at least when they feel upset. He can't remember a single positive quality or act.

DEFENSIVENESS: Defensiveness is the fighting-back response. Here the person refuses to take in anything the other person is saying. It is one arm of the typical "fight or flight" response.

Defensiveness feels like an understandable reaction to feeling besieged—this is why it is so destructive. The "victim" doesn't see anything wrong with being defensive, even though this attitude escalates a conflict rather than leading to resolution. Defensive people never say, *Maybe you're right* or *I see your point* or *Yeah, I get it. I think I owe you an apology*.

STONEWALLING: Stonewalling is the ultimate defense. The stonewaller just goes blank and withdraws from the conversation. This sends a powerful message: icy distance, superiority, and contempt.

Don't confuse stonewalling with a Time-Out. A Time-Out communicates respect. The Time-Out message is that the person cares enough about the relationship to take special efforts not to cause any further damage. And there is a very clear contract that the discussion will continue at a future time.

EMOTIONAL ABUSE & MIND GAMES

Handout

Like physical aggression, repeated emotional abuses can have severe effects on the other person's sense of self and sense of reality. These mind games sometimes leave more lasting damage than physical aggression. The person on the receiving end—male or female—may question his or her reality, feel powerless, become overdependent, etc. Here are some examples:

Coercion

- *I am going to kill myself if you leave me!*
- *Either you put out for me or I'm going to go find someone who will!*
- *I'm gonna take these kids right now, and you'll never see them again!*
- *I'll get a doctor to say you're crazy and put you away!*

Put-downs

- *You're just like your mother!*
- *My wife can't cook for shit. (in front of other people)*
- *You're stupid/You're acting crazy.*
- *There you go again—crying like a big baby.*
- *Nobody's ever going to want you!*

Isolation

- *I want to know everywhere you've been in the last 24 hours!*
- *I know you go to that school just so you can try to pick up some guy!*
- *Your family just messes you up—I don't ever want you to talk to them again!*
- *No, you can't have the car. I might need it, and you don't need to go anywhere.*
- *You can't go out. I want you to stay right at home with me.*

Blaming

- *It's your fault my career is going nowhere.*
- *Nobody else has ever made me violent! You must be doing something to cause this!*

MAY NOT BE REPRODUCED WITHOUT PERMISSION

Control

- *You don't even know how to take care of yourself without me around!*
- *You have not cleaned up this house properly!*
- *I'll decide how the money gets spent!*
- *I don't care what you think about my gambling habit—it's my money, and I'll do what I want!*
- *So what if I bought that car without discussing it with you?*

CONFLICT WITH RESPECT

◆◆◆ Handout

Arguments can be a useful way to solve problems, or they can be never-ending battles that can increase tension and the risk of abuse. The central theme here, as always, is respect. Can you offer your partner respect even when you're upset? The following guidelines can make a difference:

DANGEROUS: THE "NEGATIVE START-UP"
Why am I the only one who ever does any cleaning up around here!

It may seem true at the moment, but . . .

- it is an exaggeration of the truth.
- it does not honor the positive qualities of your partner.
- it is usually communicated in a hostile tone of voice.

INSTEAD: RULES FOR A "SOFTENED START-UP"
I know you've been really busy with the kids, but I could really use some help getting the kitchen cleaned up.

- Be concise.
- In the initial start-up complaint sentence, complain but don't blame.
- Start with something positive.
- Make statements that start with "I" instead of "you."
- Describe what is happening, but don't evaluate or judge.
- Talk clearly about what you need.
- Be polite.
- Express appreciation.
- Don't store things up.
- Restate your feelings in terms of the more vulnerable emotions.

HOW TO AVOID UNFAIR BEHAVIOR (DISRESPECT)
- Do not use name calling or put-downs.
- Do not drag up old wounds from the past.
- Stay on track; do not go off in different directions.
- Do not threaten or intimidate.
- Do not assume that you will either win or lose this argument.
- Do not save up all your gripes to dump on your partner all at once.
- Be careful of "mind-reading" self-talk. Don't assume the most negative things about your partner. ASK!
- Do not deny the facts. Come clean.
- Do not gloat over a "victory" in getting your way.
- Do not sulk, ignore, pout, withdraw, or give your partner the silent treatment.

RELATIONSHIP RESPECT CONTRACT

♦♦♦ **Handout**

We recognize that our relationship will only have a chance to be successful if none of the following behaviors take place:

1. No incidents of direct physical abuse or violence.
2. No direct or implied threats of physical abuse or violence (to self, other, or property).
3. No direct or implied threats to behave in a way that would be extremely harmful to the other person (such as exposing personal secrets).
4. No physical restrictions on either party's freedom of movement.
5. No property destruction as an expression of aggression.
6. No threats to leave the relationship (except for temporary Time-Outs to defuse tension).
7. No pattern of verbal put-downs or character assassinations or other humiliating acts.
8. No acts of infidelity or behaviors that suggest infidelity.
9. No pattern of lying or deception.
10. No pattern of abusing alcohol or drugs.

Other: _____

Both parties also agree to make all reasonable efforts to focus the therapy sessions on building the positive aspects of the relationship rather than using the session as an opportunity to simply report the bad behavior of the other party.

_____   _____
Name   Date

_____   _____
Name   Date

HOMEWORK*

◆◆◆ Handout

Practice the "softened start-up" three times. Record the results.

My "softened start-up" statement:

Response from my partner:

My "softened start-up" statement:

Response from my partner:

My "softened start-up" statement:

Response from my partner:

AND—fill out and score the *Which Attachment Style Am I?* questionnaire on the next page in preparation for the next session.

_____
*Adapted from Levine, 2010

WHICH ATTACHMENT STYLE AM I??

If TRUE, check white box—If FALSE, leave blank

Statement	A	B	C
I often worry that my partner will stop loving me.			
I find it easy to be affectionate with my partner.			
I fear that once someone gets to know the real me, he/she won't like who I am.			
I find that I bounce back quickly after a breakup. It's weird how I can just put someone out of my mind.			
When I'm not involved in a relationship, I feel somewhat anxious and incomplete.			
I find it difficult to emotionally support my partner when he/she feels down.			
When my partner is away, I'm afraid that he/she might become interested in someone else.			
I feel comfortable depending on my romantic partner.			
My independence is more important to me than my relationships.			
I prefer not to share my innermost feelings with my partner.			
When I show my partner how I feel, I'm afraid he/she will not feel the same about me.			
I am generally satisfied with my romantic relationships.			
I don't feel the need to act out much in my romantic relationships.			
I think about my relationship a lot.			
I find it difficult to depend on romantic partner.			
I tend to get very quickly attached to a romantic partner.			
I have little difficulty expressing my needs to my partner.			
I sometimes feel angry or annoyed with my partner without knowing why.			
I am very sensitive to my partner's moods.			
I believe most people are essentially honest and dependable.			
I prefer casual sex with uncommitted partners to intimate sex with one person.			
I'm comfortable sharing my personal thoughts and feelings with my partner.			

Statement	A	B	C
I worry that if my partner leaves me I might never find someone else.			
It makes me nervous when my partner gets too close.			
During a conflict, I tend to impulsively do or say things I later regret, rather than be able to reason about things.			
An argument with my partner doesn't usually cause me to question our entire relationship.			
My partners often want me to be more intimate than I feel comfortable being.			
I worry that I am not attractive enough.			
Sometimes people see me as boring because I create little drama in a relationship.			
I miss my partner when we're apart, but then when we're together I feel the need to escape.			
When I disagree with someone, I feel comfortable expressing my feelings.			
I hate that other people depend on me.			
If I notice that someone I'm interested in is checking out other people, I don't let it faze me. I might feel a pang of jealousy, but it's fleeting.			
If I notice that someone I'm interested in is checking out other people, I feel relieved--it means that he/she's not looking to make things exclusive.			
If I notice that someone I'm interested in is checking out other people, it makes me feel depressed.			
If someone I've been dating begins to act cold and distant, I may wonder what's happened, but I know it's probably not about me.			
If someone I've been dating begins to act cold and distant, I'll probably be indifferent; I might even be relieved.			
If someone I've been dating begins to act cold and distant, I'll worry that I've done something wrong.			
If my partner was to break up with me, I'd try my best to show him/her what he/she is missing (a little jealousy can't hurt).			
If someone I've been dating for several months tells me they want to stop seeing me, I'd feel hurt at first, but I'd get over it.			
Sometimes when I get what I want in a relationship, I'm not sure what I want anymore.			
I won't have much of a problem staying in touch with my ex (strictly platonic) - after all, we have a lot in common.			

Source: Levine, 2010

Add up all your checked boxes in column A: _____ Column B: _____ Column C: _____

Scoring Key: The more statements that you check in a category, the more you will display characteristics of the corresponding attachment style.

Category A—Anxious:
- You love to be very close to your partner and have the capacity for great intimacy. You often fear, however, that your partner does not wish to be as close as you would like her to be.
- Relationships tend to consume a large part of your emotional energy.
- You tend to be very sensitive to small fluctuations in your partner's moods and actions, and you sometimes take her behavior too personally.
- You experience a lot of negative emotions within the relationship and easily get upset. As a result, you tend to act out and say things you later regret.
- If the other person provides a lot of security and reassurance, you are able to let go of your preoccupation and feel contented.

Category B—Secure:
- Being warm and loving in a relationship comes naturally to you.
- You enjoy being intimate without becoming overly worried about your relationships. You take things in stride when it comes to romance and don't easily get upset over relationship matters.
- You effectively communicate your needs and feelings to your partner and are strong at reading her emotional cues and responding to them.
- You share your successes and problems with your partner, and you are able to be there in times of need.

Category C—Avoidant:
- It is very important for you to maintain your independence and self-sufficiency and you often prefer autonomy to intimate relationships.
- Even though you do want to be close to others, you feel uncomfortable with too much closeness and tend to keep your partner at arm's length.
- You don't spend much time worrying about your romantic relationships or about being rejected.
- You tend not to open up to your partner, and she often complains that you are emotionally distant.
- In relationships, you are often on high alert for any signs of control or impingement on your territory by your partner.

CAN I COUNT ON YOU?

Handout

Everyone walks around with doubts and insecurities about their intimate relationships. Here's a list of typical worries that people carry around—can you count on reassuring answers to these questions in your relationship? Can your partner count on reassuring answers from you?

- *Will I be physically safe?*
- *Do I really matter to you enough that you'll put me first when it really counts—before your job, before your friends, even before your family?*
- *Can I count on you to give me space when I need it?*
- *Do I have to worry about you abandoning me?*
- *Do I have to worry about competing with someone else?*
- *Can I trust you not to hurt or humiliate me?*
- *Do I have to worry about your threats?*
- *Can I count on the fact that I really know you?*
- *Are you really paying attention to who I am and not who you imagine or want me to be? Can I be myself with you?*
- *Can I count on you to act like an adult?*
- *Do you really value me/cherish me? Can I count on you to consistently let me know how important I am to you?*

EFFECTIVE COMMUNICATION*

♦ Handout

Situation	Ineffective Communication (Protest behavior)	Effective Communication
She's very busy at work and you hardly get to see her.	Call her every couple of hours to make sure you're on her mind.	Tell her you miss her and are having a hard time adjusting to her new work schedule, even though you understand that it's temporary.
She doesn't really listen to you when you're talking, which makes you feel unimportant and misunderstood.	Get up in the middle of the conversation and go to another room (hoping she will follow you and apologize).	Make it clear that it's not enough that she listens without responding. Emphasize that you value her opinion above anyone's and it's important to you to know what she thinks.
She talks about her ex-boyfriend, which makes you feel insecure.	Tell her it's pathetic that she's still talking about her ex, or.. Bring up other girls you went out with to let her know how bad it feels.	Let her know that conversations about her ex-boyfriend make you feel inadequate and unsure of where you stand, that you need to feel secure in order to be happy with someone.
She always changes plans at the last minute.	Do the same thing to her so eventually she'll learn how it feels.	Explain that you feel unsettled not being able to count on plans with her and that it's better for you to at least have a ballpark schedule most of the time.

It's important to remember that even with effective communication, some problems won't be solved immediately. What's vital is your partner's response—whether she is concerned about your well-being, has your best interest in mind, and is willing to work on things.

*Levine, 2010

HOMEWORK

♦ Handout

Fill out the *Which Attachment Style Am I?* questionnaire, but this time answering as if you are your partner. See if it helps you understand her better and why certain situations activate her fears.

WHICH ATTACHMENT STYLE AM I?? If TRUE, check white box—If FALSE, leave blank	TRUE A	TRUE B	TRUE C
I often worry that my partner will stop loving me.			
I find it easy to be affectionate with my partner.			
I fear that once someone gets to know the real me, he/she won't like who I am.			
I find that I bounce back quickly after a breakup. It's weird how I can just put someone out of my mind.			
When I'm not involved in a relationship, I feel somewhat anxious and incomplete.			
I find it difficult to emotionally support my partner when he/she feels down.			
When my partner is away, I'm afraid that he/she might become interested in someone else.			
I feel comfortable depending on my romantic partner.			
My independence is more important to me than my relationships.			
I prefer not to share my innermost feelings with my partner.			
When I show my partner how I feel, I'm afraid he/she will not feel the same about me.			
I am generally satisfied with my romantic relationships.			
I don't feel the need to act out much in my romantic relationships.			
I think about my relationship a lot.			
I find it difficult to depend on romantic partner.			

MAY NOT BE REPRODUCED WITHOUT PERMISSION

I tend to get very quickly attached to a romantic partner.			
I have little difficulty expressing my needs to my partner.			
I sometimes feel angry or annoyed with my partner without knowing why.			
I am very sensitive to my partner's moods.			
I believe most people are essentially honest and dependable.			
I prefer casual sex with uncommitted partners to intimate sex with one person.			
I'm comfortable sharing my personal thoughts and feelings with my partner.			
I worry that if my partner leaves me I might never find someone else.			
It makes me nervous when my partner gets too close.			
During a conflict, I tend to impulsively do or say things I later regret, rather than be able to reason about things.			
An argument with my partner doesn't usually cause me to question our entire relationship.			
My partners often want me to be more intimate than I feel comfortable being.			
I worry that I am not attractive enough.			
Sometimes people see me as boring because I create little drama in a relationship.			
I miss my partner when we're apart, but then when we're together I feel the need to escape.			
When I disagree with someone, I feel comfortable expressing my feelings.			
I hate that other people depend on me.			
If I notice that someone I'm interested in is checking out other people, I don't let it faze me. I might feel a pang of jealousy, but it's fleeting.			
If I notice that someone I'm interested in is checking out other people, I feel relieved--it means that he/she's not looking to make things exclusive.			
If I notice that someone I'm interested in is checking out other people, it makes me feel depressed.			

If someone I've been dating begins to act cold and distant, I may wonder what's happened, but I know it's probably not about me.			
If someone I've been dating begins to act cold and distant, I'll probably be indifferent; I might even be relieved.			
If someone I've been dating begins to act cold and distant, I'll worry that I've done something wrong.			
If my partner was to break up with me, I'd try my best to show him/her what he/she is missing (a little jealousy can't hurt).			
If someone I've been dating for several months tells me they want to stop seeing me, I'd feel hurt at first, but I'd get over it.			
Sometimes when I get what I want in a relationship, I'm not sure what I want anymore.			
I won't have much of a problem staying in touch with my ex (strictly platonic) - after all, we have a lot in common.			

Source: Levine, A., & Heller, R. (2010). *Attached*. London: Rodale

Add up all your checked boxes in column A: _____ Column B: _____ Column C: _____

Scoring Key: The more statements that you check in a category, the more you will display characteristics of the corresponding attachment style.

Category A—Anxious

Category B—Secure

Category C—Avoidant

THE ART OF APOLOGIES

♦♦♦ Handout

Apologies grease the wheels of most successful relationships. The art of delivering a sincere and well-timed apology is one that all of us should be very skilled at.

The obvious trigger situation for an apology is when you realize that you have done something that has hurt someone you care about. Even if your action was not intended to hurt or you were not aware of how it would affect the other person, an apology is still in order.

To apologize successfully, you need to have a solid "platform of self-worth" to stand on so you will not collapse into shame. The more self-worth you have, the more you can handle the ego blow offering an apology—because admitting mistakes does not make you a doomed or despicable person. Just an imperfect one.

An effective apology requires four distinct elements to make it more likely to be well-received (which is, after all, the point of the apology in the first place):

1. THE BASIC STATEMENT: "I'm sorry." No rationalizations, no excuses, no hedging. Just a simple statement that you are sorry and what you are sorry for having done. It could be big or very minor, it doesn't matter.

Start by describing exactly what you did wrong, then just acknowledge that this was a mistake. Accept responsibility:

- *I'm really sorry I started teasing you in front of your friends.*
- *I feel terrible for having that affair and I am really, really sorry for how I have hurt you!*
- *Sorry I forgot to make that bill payment.*

Remember to get your BUT out of your apology: A BUT might sound like this: *I'm sorry I yelled at you, but you weren't listening to me.* This signals a rationalization, an excuse, and a focus on the other person's behaviors. Just stick with *I'm sorry I yelled at you.*

While often your partner may have pieces to apologize for, a true apology only focuses on your behaviors. Take ownership of your part, find out how it impacted the other person, and begin to repair.

2. DEMONSTRATION OF INSIGHT: You need to offer the other person some evidence that you have learned something or that there was some temporary circumstance that will not happen again, or at least that you will really be on guard against it the next time around:

- *I think I was just feeling insecure, and this was some sort of way to make jokes and fit in! I won't let that happen again.*
- *There's no excuse—it had everything to do with me and my feeling like I'm not getting enough attention. I wish there was some way I could go back in time and talk to you about what I've been going through instead of doing what I did!*
- *I was really rushing around last night, and I didn't pay attention. I'm going to start writing it in my appointment book to make sure I remember each month.*

3. DEMONSTRATION OF EMPATHY: You need to make it as clear as possible that you really understand the pain or anxiety or mistrust that your actions have created in your partner: *I realize now how hurt you feel and how hard it is for you trust me again. I get it now—or at least I'm trying to.*

You need to make sure that you have listened to your partner's pain and that you clearly communicate the following message: *I want you to know that this is NOT going to slip out of my head.*

4. BEHAVIOR CHANGE: The proof is in the pudding. All the words and all the good intentions in the world don't mean a thing unless your partner sees, over time, that you have genuinely learned something from your mistake and that you are handling the situations differently. Maybe not 100% perfectly, but definitely better. Remember that your partner cannot possibly feel secure until he or she has observed, over time, that you have changed. Obviously, the length of time this takes is directly related to how serious the "crime" was.

CLASSIC APOLOGY MISTAKES

◆◆◆ **Handout**

1. **Not being genuine.** How do you like it when you hear *I'm sorry you feel that way* or *I'm sorry if that hurt your feelings*? Sometimes that might be ok, but most of the time this does not show sincere regret. In fact, it often makes your partner feel stupid for "overreacting" or being "too sensitive." This usually does not get a passing grade as a genuine apology.

2. **Crummy body language.** Maybe the words are right, but there is no eye contact or there is a hostile look. Or the tone of voice sounds sarcastic. This also fails the grade.

3. **Waiting for the perfect moment. It is never too late to apologize.** Some people wait for the "perfect moment" for an apology. This does not exist (although it's probably best not to do it in heavy traffic or when the baby is screaming). The perfect moment to apologize is the moment you realize you've done something wrong or as soon as possible thereafter.

4. **Getting defensive** (See *Nondefensive Listening* below): Often we listen for the part of the criticisms or anger that we don't agree with or for some minor flaw in the person's story of what happened, or we try to think of some time when the other person treated us this way or of a reason the other person was oversensitive—anything to deflect from the simple responsibility of recognizing a mistake and apologizing for it.

5. **Not listening carefully.** Apologizing is much more than offering the words *I am sorry*. While these words mark the beginning, it is a process that can sometimes feel like a long-distance run. At the core of an honest and authentic apology is the ability to listen. You must be willing to sit with your partner's anger and pain. You need to stay there long enough to really grasp the injury and to validate the feelings.

6. **Expecting immediate and total forgiveness.** Remember commandment #5: *We do not have control over any other person, but we do have control over ourselves*. All you can do is give it your best and most sincere shot. Your partner may never be able to forgive you, or it may just take a while.

7. **Apologizing too much.** Some people apologize way too much, for the smallest things, or even when they haven't really done anything wrong. This is just plain irritating, and it's like crying wolf. The real and significant apologies will be weakened if excessive apologies become annoying or are designed to make the partner feel sorry for the apologizer.

HANDLING CRITICISM: NONDEFENSIVE LISTENING

Handout

When someone approaches you in an angry or critical way, it is tempting to listen for what you don't agree with and to get defensive. It's so automatic that it takes motivation, courage, and goodwill to observe your defensiveness and practice stepping aside from it.

NONDEFENSIVE LISTENING is at the heart of offering a sincere apology. Here are 12 points to keep in mind when you're on the receiving end of criticism.

1. **RECOGNIZE YOUR DEFENSIVENESS.** We are wired to go immediately into defensive mode when criticized. Becoming aware of your defensiveness can give you a tiny, but crucial, bit of distance from it. Catch yourself when you are focusing on the inaccuracies, distortions, and exaggerations that will inevitably be there.

2. **BREATHE.** Defensiveness starts in the body, making us tense and on guard and unable to take in new information. Do what you can to calm yourself. Take slow and deep breaths.

3. **LISTEN ONLY TO UNDERSTAND.** Listen only to discover what you can agree with. Do not interrupt, argue, refute or correct facts, or bring up your own criticisms and complaints. If your points are legitimate, that's all the more reason to save them for a different conversation, when they can be a focus of conversation and not a defense strategy.

4. **ASK QUESTIONS.** Look for clarity about whatever you don't understand. When the criticism is vague (*You don't respect me*), ask for a concrete example (*Can you give me another example where you felt I was putting you down?*). This will add to your clarity and show your partner that you care about understanding him or her. Note: Asking for specifics is not the same thing as nitpicking—the key is to be curious, not to cross-examine. Don't act like a lawyer (even if you are one).

6. **APOLOGIZE FOR YOUR PART.** You may only agree with seven percent of what your partner is saying (*I think you're right that I was totally hogging the conversation the other night*), but acknowledge that part. It will indicate to your partner that you're capable of taking responsibility, not just evading it. It will also help shift the exchange out of combat into collaboration. Save your thoughts about their part until later.

7. **ACKNOWLEDGE THE COMPLAINT.** Let your partner know he or she has been heard and that you will continue to think about the conversation. Even if nothing has been resolved, tell your partner that he or she has reached you. (*It's not easy to hear what you're telling me, but I want you to know that I'm going to give it a lot of thought.*) Take time to genuinely consider your partner's point of view.

8. **THANK YOUR PARTNER for sharing feelings.** It works best to express gratitude where the other person might expect mere defensiveness (*I appreciate your telling me this. I know it couldn't have been easy*).

9. **INITIATE THE FOLLOW-UP CONVERSATION.** Show your partner that you're continuing to think about his or her point of view and that you're willing to revisit the issue (*I've been thinking about our conversation last week, and I'm really glad that we had that talk, even if it was hard for me to hear. I'm wondering if there's more you haven't told me.*).

10. **DRAW THE LINE AT INSULTS.** There may be a time to sit through an initial blast, but not if rudeness has become a pattern in your relationship rather than an uncommon occurrence. Exit from rudeness while offering the possibility of another conversation (*I want to hear what bothers you, but I need you to approach me with respect*).

11. **DON'T LISTEN WHEN YOU CAN'T LISTEN WELL.** It's fine to tell your partner that you want to have the conversation and that you recognize its importance, but you can't have it right now. If you're closing the conversation, suggest a specific window of time to resume it (*I can't absorb what you're saying now. Let's come back to it tomorrow when I'll be able to give you my full attention*).

12. **DEFINE YOUR DIFFERENCES.** At some point, you may need to tell your partner how you see things differently rather than being an overly accommodating, peace-at-any-price type of person who apologizes to avoid conflict. Even if your partner isn't able to consider your point of view, you may need to hear the sound of your own voice saying what you really think. Timing is crucial, so consider saving your different point of view for a future conversation when you'll have the best chance of being heard.

Excerpted from Lerner, H. (2017). *Why Won't You Apologize? Healing Big Betrayals and Everyday Hurts* New York: Touchstone.

HOMEWORK

Handout

Identify three apologies you could offer to your wife or partner or children. Deliver each apology, and record the response from each person. If you are not in contact with any of them, identify three apologies you would make if you had the opportunity.

1. Apology from you:

   Response from wife, partner, or child:

   _

2. Apology from you:

   Response from wife, partner, or child:

   _

3. Apology from you:

   Response from wife, partner, or child:

MAY NOT BE REPRODUCED WITHOUT PERMISSION

SEXUAL ABUSE: PSYCHOLOGICAL AND PHYSICAL

Handout

Sexual abuse is one of the rooms in the *House of Abuse* that is especially difficult to talk about. Sometimes it is even difficult to know that it is taking place. Below are examples of different forms of abusive sexual behaviors, both psychological and physical. If you can, try to be honest with yourself about which of these you may have used at some point in your relationships.

PUT-DOWNS:
- *Making jokes about women in your wife's or partner's presence*
- *Checking out other women in her presence*
- *Making sexual put-down jokes*
- *Comparing her body to those of other women or to pictures in magazines*
- *Criticizing sexual performance*
- *Blaming her if you don't feel satisfied with sex*
- *Using sexual labels: calling her a "slut" or "frigid"*

MIND GAMES:
- *Telling her that agreeing to sex is the only way she can prove she has been faithful or that she still loves you*
- *Revealing intimate details about her to others*
- *Withholding sex and affection only to gain control over her*
- *Engaging in sexual affairs (and lying about it)*

PRESSURE:
- *Expecting sex whenever you want it*
- *Demanding sex with threats*
- *Pressuring her into stripping or talking sexually in a way that feels humiliating to her*
- *Pressuring her into watching sex or pornography when this is offensive to her*
- *Pressuring her into touching others when this is offensive to her*

FORCE:
- *Forcing sex while she's sleeping or intoxicated*
- *Touching her in ways that are uncomfortable to her*
- *Forcing uncomfortable sex*
- *Forcing sex after physical abuse*
- *Sex that hurts her (use of objects/weapons) without her consent*

MASCULINITY TRAPS: SEX*

◆◆◆ Handout

MASCULINITY TRAPS	THE BIG PICTURE
I deserve to have sex upon demand	Sex involves the needs of two people, not just one.
If my wife or partner doesn't put out, it means she's trying to hurt me	There are many reasons why she may not be in the mood for sex
Real men get laid all the time	Many men talk big—real men respect the individuality of the woman they love
I've had a hard day. I deserve some rewards	I can't expect her to always be available exactly when I need her.

*Adapted with permission from Larance et al., 2009.

ABOUT SEX

◆ Handout

Sex has different meanings to each person. Some people view sex as a way to connect with another individual on a more intimate level. Some view sex as an extension of their love. Others may view sex as an outlet for stress and tension. The following is meant to help you clarify YOUR definition of sex, and your values, feelings, and expectations when you are sexually intimate with someone.

- *I feel attractive to my partner when . . .*
- *When my partner rejects me sexually, I (include feelings and actions) . . .*
- *When I don't feel like being sexually intimate, I . . .*
- *After having sex, I feel . . .*
- *I think masturbation is . . .*
- *A time I regret having sex (include why) . . .*
- *A time I used sex to get what I wanted was . . .*
- *I feel used sexually when . . .*
- *Sex after an argument is . . .*
- *Refusing sex to punish a partner is . . .*
- *It is ok/not ok for me to cheat sexually on my partner because . . .*
- *A person in a relationship should/should not flirt (include why) . . .*
- *I think that women think sex is . . .*
- *What I like most about sex with my partner is . . .*
- *What I like least about sex with my partner is . . .*
- *If I want to have sex and my partner doesn't, I usually . . .*

MAY NOT BE REPRODUCED WITHOUT PERMISSION

HOMEWORK

◆◆◆ Handout

Based on your own life experience, prepare three messages or words of advice you would want to pass on to your son (or what you would suggest a father should pass on to his son, or what you wish your father had said to you) about how to handle sex in a meaningful relationship.

1.

2.

3.

QUESTIONS FOR KIDS

◆◆◆◆ **Handout**

In this exercise, group members take turns playing the role of the child in their house who has witnessed violence. Other group members interview these "kids" about their experiences.

1. What kinds of things do your mom and dad fight about?
2. What happens when your mom or dad gets angry or your parents fight? Can you describe any fights between your parents that you saw yourself? What did you see or hear during the fight? What was it like for you afterward (e.g., did you see your parents' injuries or the house torn apart)? What were your reactions?
3. What do you do if your parents push, shove, or hit each other? Do you leave the room or go outside?
4. Can you describe any fights between your parents in which you were caught in the middle, or when you tried to stop them? What happened?
5. Do they ever fight about you? How does this make you feel (scared, confused, sad, mad)?
6. Do you talk to anybody about this?
7. How do you handle your feelings since this has happened? Do you ever feel like hurting yourself or anyone else?
8. In an emergency for you or your parents, who would you call? Where could you go?

HOMEWORK

◆◆◆ **Handout**

Complete the following *Kid Stories* exercise and bring it for group review next session.

    1. You are an 8-year-old boy, and you like playing video games more than anything else. Your dad has been getting drunk lately. He comes home and hits your mom, and he breaks things after he thinks the kids have gone to sleep. Your older sister has started using drugs and running away. One day after school, your mom says you're all going to be moving away from your dad, with her, to another town across the state, near your aunt and uncle. Your mom tells you that she can't trust your dad anymore and that you kids might be the next to get hurt. You've never seen your dad hit your sister, and he's never hit you.

How would you feel when you heard about your mom's plans?

How would you feel toward her?

How would you feel toward your father?

    2. You are a 10-year-old girl who's been really screwing up at school lately. Your dad is constantly on your case; it seems like nothing you do is right. You know your mom has been spending a lot of money, and he is always yelling at her about it. One time he locked her out of the house, and she had to stay outside in the rain until you snuck around the back to let her in. She yells right back at him, calling him bad names. Sometimes she even throws things at him and you can hear things breaking. You and your mom have left a couple of times for a few days, but she always comes back. It's hard for you to sleep. You want this to stop, and you ask if you can live with somebody else for a while.

How would you feel toward your mother?

How would you feel toward your father?

ACCOUNTABILITY STATEMENT*

◆◆◆◆ Handout

We are making an assumption here that all of you want the best for your relationship and do not want to be in an abusive or destructive relationship. But something seems to come along and bring out behaviors in you that you thought you would never do.

We want to help you figure out what you told yourself when you acted aggressively that somehow made it seem right or fair at the time.

When you figure this out, you become more powerful. And you become more fully accountable for your own actions. When you know what to look for, you are more likely to act like the man you really want to be.

ACCOUNTABILITY DEFENSES

◆◆ Handout

Most people who behave destructively towards their partner find a way to justify it in their own minds. Even though they do not usually believe in being abusive towards a family member or partner, in certain situations they "make an exception."

Then, afterwards, they figure out some way to make it OK, rather than simply saying the obvious: *I blew it. I crossed over a line, and it's nobody's fault but my own.*

Here are some typical examples of ways people try to make their behavior OK.

NO BIG DEAL: *I wasn't violent; all I did was slap her.*

INTENTION: *I didn't mean to hurt her—I just wanted her to understand!*

SELF-EXPRESSION: *It was my turn to let her know what I've been going through!*

INTOXICATION/LOSS OF CONTROL: *I was drunk; what can I say? I just flipped out; I didn't even know what I was doing.*

PROJECTION OF BLAME: *It's her fault; if she hadn't pushed me, or nagged me, or spent too much money . . .*

DISTORTION OF ROLE: *I had to get physical with her for her own good—she was acting so crazy!*

MAY NOT BE REPRODUCED WITHOUT PERMISSION

THE WAY AGGRESSIVE PEOPLE THINK

◆◆◆ Handout

Research about violent and criminal behavior has identified attitudes that make it way more likely for people to act aggressively. These are called "aggressive beliefs." And the same is true for many people who end up acting aggressively in their intimate partner relationships.

As we go through these, see how many of these attitudes you can spot in yourself—and also try to understand where these came from and how they may actually have been useful at certain times in your life.

1. *VIOLENCE IS NORMAL*

   You think that . . .

   - Violence resolves conflicts.
   - Violence persuades others to do things.
   - Violence can be exhilarating or simply makes you feel better.
   - Violence makes others treat you with respect.
   - Violence is both acceptable and effective with little or no lasting negative consequences.

   Here's what people who think like this often say:

   - *She'll get over it, it's no big deal.*
   - *When I was a child, yeah, I got a beating, but it wasn't anything—it was good for me.*
   - *She wouldn't listen to me unless I her/him first.*
   - *This happens in a lot of families—no big deal.*
   - *How else was I going to get through to her that paying attention to me was important?*
   - *I told her this would happen if she came home late again.*

2. *I AM THE LAW*

   - You act like the "local sheriff": you believe that you can identify when violence is needed and that you are well qualified to deliver it.
   - You assume a position of moral leadership in your family or community and use violence to enforce it.

   Here's what people who think like this often say:

   - *People come to me with their problems because they know they can rely on me to sort them out.*
   - *My niece phoned me up. Her partner had been hitting her. She'd been asking me what she should do. I said, "just throw him out" but she said, "I can't, it's my baby's father." So, me and him had a fight. I went a bit overboard; my niece got really mad at me. She called the police. I was really hurt that she did that, after she asked for my help.*

3. *BEAT OR BE BEATEN*

   - You see yourself as victim.
   - You feel forced into violence by the intent of others to prey on you.
   - You believe YOU must make the first move—or else you will be assaulted or disrespected.

MAY NOT BE REPRODUCED WITHOUT PERMISSION

Here's what people who think like this often say:

- *She was testing me—if I hadn't sorted it out then, it would just have got worse.*
- *If I get ripped off, people will think that they can get away with it. It has got to stop.*
- *I don't like hurting her, but what choice have I got? She'll walk all over me.*

4. *I KNOW VIOLENCE IS A PROBLEM, BUT . . . I JUST GET OUT OF CONTROL*

- You perceive yourself to be incapable of self-regulation.
- You hold other people responsible when you get out of control.

Here's what people who think like this often say:

- *She shouldn't have done that to me.*
- *She knows how I am when . . .*
- *I know once she challenges me I'm going to get violent, it just can't be helped.*
- *All of a sudden I go on a rage.*
- *I was drunk; what can I say?*
- *I only meant to let her know she couldn't get away with that shit. But once I started, my kids had to pull me off her. That's just how it is sometimes with me.*

ACCOUNTABILITY CHECKLIST*

♦♦♦ Handout

As you fill out this form, remember Commandment #1: *We are all 100% responsible for our own actions*. **You will not be turning this in**, but we will review this in group.

We are not asking you to admit to something that you did not do nor to take responsibility for something that someone else has done.

I have acted in the following destructive ways toward my partner. (Circle each):

Verbal abuse	Controlling partner	Intimidation	Mind games
Property destruction	Manipulating kids	Threats	Forced sex
Put-downs	Stalking	Monitoring mail/phones	Sexual put-downs
Isolation of partner	Controlling $	Ignore/Withdraw	Affairs
Physical restraint	Pushing	Slapping	Kicking
Throwing things	Choking	Use of weapons	Other

Other:_____

- I take responsibility for these destructive behaviors. My behavior was not *caused* by my partner. I had a choice.

- I have used the following to rationalize my destructive behaviors in this relationship (e.g., *she was nagging me, I felt disrespected, I just can't control myself when she does that,* etc.)

    1.

    2.

    3.

- I recognize that my partner may be distrustful, intimidated, and fearful of me because of these behaviors.

---

*Adapted with permission from Pence & Paymar, 1993.

HOMEWORK

◆◆◆ Handout

Record three examples of the way aggressive people think that you notice in the next week or that you can remember from the past. These can be in your own thinking, the thinking of someone you know, or even the thinking of a character in a movie or TV show. Name the category that this represents.

1. Attitude/Thinking pattern:

   Which category is this an example of?

   VIOLENCE IS NORMAL _____

   I AM THE LAW _____

   BEAT OR BE BEATEN _____

   I KNOW VIOLENCE IS A PROBLEM, BUT . . . I JUST GET OUT OF CONTROL _____

- -

2. Attitude/Thinking pattern:

   Which category is this an example of?

   VIOLENCE IS NORMAL _____

   I AM THE LAW _____

   BEAT OR BE BEATEN _____

   I KNOW VIOLENCE IS A PROBLEM, BUT . . . I JUST GET OUT OF CONTROL _____

- -

3. Attitude/Thinking pattern:

   Which category is this an example of?

   VIOLENCE IS NORMAL _____

   I AM THE LAW _____

   BEAT OR BE BEATEN _____

   I KNOW VIOLENCE IS A PROBLEM, BUT . . . I JUST GET OUT OF CONTROL _____

STAKE IN CONFORMITY: PROTECT WHAT YOU'VE EARNED!

◆ Handout

Protect the investments made in your family, life, career, and relationships—You have worked too hard not to! –U.S. Marine Corps

One thing that stops people from crossing the line into violent behavior is a fear of losing something important.

But to fear loss, people must feel like they actually have something to lose. Research shows that arrest only works for men with something to lose by being arrested. Men arrested for domestic violence with high levels of *stake in conformity* are less likely to reassault their partners after being arrested.

Which of the following are true for you?

1. Employed more than 12 months steadily
2. Lived in the same residence 12 months
3. 25 years old or older
4. Married
5. Actively parenting a child or children
6. You have a biological child with partner (living with the two of you at the time of the assault)
7. You have NOT served jail time other than for the current offense
8. You are a member of a family, religious community, workplace, or other social group that disapproves of domestic violence

The higher your score, the greater the likelihood that you have a high *stake in conformity* and are less likely to commit any future acts of violence or aggression.

POTENTIAL LOSSES: How painful (10 extremely painful, 0 not painful) would it be if, because of your domestic violence, you . . .

1. Lost your job _____
2. Lost your relationship _____
3. Lost access to your children _____
4. Served time in jail _____
5. Had to face your parents and other family members _____
6. Had to face your employer and coworkers _____
7. Had to face your friends _____
8. Had to face your church or religious group _____

SCREW YOU!

◆◆◆ **Handout**

This is a description of a counseling session (adapted from an interview with Terrence Real, 2012) with a woman who described herself as a "rage-aholic." She would go off on her husband in wild verbal rages (never quite physical) in front of their kids, saying really insulting and damaging things that left everyone feeling wounded and scared.

She hated herself afterwards and was seeking help to get more self-control. Here's how the counseling session went:

Counselor: *You have to stop doing this.*

She said, as most ragers do: *It comes up on me too quickly. I can't.*

Then the counselor made a strategic move: *OK, here's what I want you to do. Do you have pictures of your kids?*

She got out her phone and showed him some pictures.

Counselor: *OK, you have my permission to rage at your husband in front of your kids. But before you do that, I want you to look at some family photos of your kids and look into their eyes and say, "I know what I'm about to do is going to cause you deep and permanent harm, but right now, my anger is more important to me than you are, so screw you."*

He put his arm around her shoulder and said: *Let's practice that. Hold up the pictures, and say . . .*

She burst into tears: *I can't say that to my children.*

He said: *No, but you ARE saying that to your children. You're saying that each time you scream at their father in front of them. All I want you to do is say it out loud and own it.*

Then she said: *I'll never rage at my husband again for the rest of my life.*

HOMEWORK

◆◆◆ Handout

Identify eight things that you stand to lose if you become abusive or violent with your partner again. The more of these you can come up with, the greater your "stake in conformity."

1.
2.
3.
4.
5.
6.
7.
8.

AND fill out the *MAST* questionnaire below and score in preparation for next session:

The MICHIGAN ALCOHOL SCREENING TEST (MAST)

1. Do you feel like a normal drinker? ("normal" = drink as much or less than most people)
   Circle answer: YES   NO

2. Have you ever awakened the morning after some drinking the night before and found that you could not remember part of the evening?
   Circle answer: YES   NO

3. Does any near relative or close friend ever worry or complain about your drinking?
   Circle answer: YES   NO

4. Can you stop drinking without difficulty after one or two drinks?
   Circle answer: YES   NO

5. Do you ever feel guilty about your drinking?
   Circle answer: YES   NO

6. Have you ever attended a meeting of Alcoholics Anonymous (AA)?
   Circle answer: YES   NO

MAY NOT BE REPRODUCED WITHOUT PERMISSION

7. Have you ever gotten into physical fights when drinking?

   Circle answer: YES   NO

8. Has drinking ever created problems between you and a near relative or close friend?

   Circle answer: YES   NO

9. Has any family member or close friend gone to anyone for help about your drinking?

   Circle answer: YES   NO

10. Have you ever lost friends because of your drinking?

    Circle answer: YES   NO

11. Have you ever gotten into trouble at work because of drinking?

    Circle answer: YES   NO

12. Have you ever lost a job because of your drinking?

    Circle answer: YES   NO

13. Have you ever neglected your obligations, your family, or your work for two or more days in a row because you were drinking?

    Circle answer: YES   NO

14. Do you drink before noon fairly often?

    Circle answer: YES   NO

15. Have you ever been told you have liver trouble such as cirrhosis?

    Circle answer: YES   NO

16. After heavy drinking have you ever had delirium tremens (DT), severe shaking, visual or auditory (hearing) hallucinations?

    Circle answer: YES   NO

17. Have you ever gone to anyone for help about your drinking?

    Circle answer: YES   NO

18. Have you ever been hospitalized because of your drinking?

    Circle answer: YES   NO

19. Has your drinking ever resulted in you being hospitalized in a psychiatric ward?

    Circle answer: YES   NO

20. Have you ever gone to any doctor, social worker, clergyman, or mental health clinic for help with any emotional problem in which drinking was part?

Circle answer: YES   NO

21. Have you been arrested more than once for driving under the influence of alcohol?

Circle answer: YES   NO

22. Have you ever been arrested, even for a few hours, because of other behavior while drinking?

Circle answer: YES   NO

Please score one point if you answered the following:

1. No
2. Yes
3. Yes
4. No
5. Yes
6. Yes

7 through 22. Yes

Add up the scores and compare to the following score card:

0 – 2 = No apparent problem
3 – 5 = Early or middle problem drinker
6 or more = Problem drinker

I REALLY DIDN'T MEAN TO DO IT . . . I WAS DRUNK

❖❖❖ **Handout**

Some people who hurt the ones they love have problems with alcohol. Some also have problems with other drugs, such as pot, crystal meth, and cocaine. People under the influence often impulsively do things they may not ordinarily do, and their judgment and control are impaired.

This session is about taking responsibility for all of your decisions and actions, including using substances.

People use chemicals for many different reasons. On the questionnaires that follow, think about the reasons you use alcohol or drugs. Then, identify whether substances impair your judgment or causes you to become aggressive.

And ask yourself these questions as you think about the ways drugs or alcohol may be hurting your relationship:

- *Have you ever done something while under the influence that you regretted afterward?*
- *Have you ever become more abusive or aggressive when using alcohol or drugs?*
- *Have you missed work/school due to your use?*
- *Were most of your "bad" choices made while you were under the influence?*
- *Have you ever tried to cut back on your drinking or drug use?*
- *Has anyone ever been annoyed about your drinking or told you that you have a substance abuse problem?*
- *Have you ever experienced memory lapses or blackouts?*

Any "yes" answers indicate that alcohol or drug use has probably impaired your ability to be fully in control of your life. Remember the 100% rule regarding responsibility. Alcohol and drug problems are usually progressive—without help, they get worse. Can you really be 100% committed to being in control of your life and still continue to abuse alcohol or drugs?

MAY NOT BE REPRODUCED WITHOUT PERMISSION

WHY DO WE CARE?: THE RELATIONSHIP BETWEEN SUBSTANCE ABUSE AND INTIMATE PARTNER VIOLENCE*

Handout

- 60% of domestic violence incidents involve perpetrators who have been drinking.

- The likelihood of male to female aggression is 8 times higher on days when the perpetrator was drinking alcohol.

- Binge drinking is especially closely associated with partner abuse. Binge drinking is defined as consuming five or more standard drinks in one sitting at least once in a 30-day period. Individuals who engage in binge drinking are 5 times more likely to have interpersonal conflicts with their partner and engage in aggressive behavior.

- Alcohol intoxication can lead to negative feelings such as depression, helplessness, and hopelessness. Being depressed significantly increases the likelihood of intimate partner violence.

- Over 50% of alcoholics have been violent toward a female partner in the year before beginning alcoholism treatment.

---

*Information provided by Donald Meichenbaum, Ph.D.

HOMEWORK

◆◆ Handout

Just for one week, keep track of how much alcohol you consume. Make notes of the day, the time of day, the situation, and the number of drinks. Remember that "one drink" is defined as one 6 oz. glass of wine, one 12 oz. beer, or 1 ½ oz. hard liquor.

AND fill out the *Safe At Home Questionnaire, Revised* and score it in preparation for the next session.

SAFE AT HOME QUESTIONNAIRE, REVISED

Instructions: Please circle the number that BEST describes how much you agree or disagree with each statement listed below.

Item #	Item Statement	I Strongly Agree	I Agree	I Don't Agree or Disagree	I Disagree	I Strongly Disagree
1-C	The last time I lost control of myself, I realized that I have a problem.	1	2	3	4	5
2-M	I do not believe that I will return to my old ways of losing control.	1	2	3	4	5
3-P/A	I try to listen carefully to others so that I don't get into conflicts anymore.	1	2	3	4	5
4-C	It feels good to finally face how I've been messing up my life.	1	2	3	4	5
5-P	It's no big deal if I lose my temper from time to time.	1	2	3	4	5
6 P/A	I handle it safely when people get angry with me.	1	2	3	4	5
7-*	Sometimes I find that it is still very hard for me to avoid my old ways of treating my partner.	1	2	3	4	5
8-*	I have a problem with losing control of myself.	1	2	3	4	5
9-C	I want to do something about my problem with conflict.	1	2	3	4	5
10-C	I want help with my temper.	1	2	3	4	5
11-P	I'll come to groups but I won't talk.	1	2	3	4	5
12 P/A	I am actively keeping my cool when my partner(s) and I have conflicts.	1	2	3	4	5
13-C	I need to change before it's too late.	1	2	3	4	5

14-P	There's nothing wrong with the way I handle situations but I get into trouble for it anyway.	1	2	3	4	5
15 P/A	Even though I get angry I know ways to avoid losing control of myself.	1	2	3	4	5
16-M	I really am different now than I was when conflicts were a problem for me.	1	2	3	4	5
17-C	I guess I need help with the way I handle things.	1	2	3	4	5
18-P	It'll cost me plenty to get help.	1	2	3	4	5
19-M	I have been successful at keeping myself from going back to my old ways of acting when I have conflicts with my partner.	1	2	3	4	5
20-P	If my partner doesn't like the way I act, it's just too bad.	1	2	3	4	5
21-C	Some of what I see and hear about people being abusive seems to apply with me.	1	2	3	4	5
22 -P/A	When I feel myself getting upset I have ways to keep myself from getting into trouble.	1	2	3	4	5
23-C	I'm sick of screwing up my life.	1	2	3	4	5
24-M	I try to talk things out with others so that I don't get into conflicts anymore.	1	2	3	4	5
25-M	I am sure that I will never return to my old ways of treating my partner(s).	1	2	3	4	5
26-P	It's my partner's fault that I act this way.	1	2	3	4	5
27-*	It's okay that I got into trouble because it means that now I'm getting help.	1	2	3	4	5
28-P/A	It's becoming more natural for me to be in control of myself.	1	2	3	4	5
29-P	I'd get help if I had more free time.	1	2	3	4	5
30-P/A	I have a plan for what I do when I feel upset.	1	2	3	4	5
31-*	Recent changes that I have made probably won't last.	1	2	3	4	5
32-C	It's time for me to listen to people telling me that I need help.	1	2	3	4	5
33-M	I know the early cues for when I'm losing control.	1	2	3	4	5
34-P	I need to control my partner.	1	2	3	4	5

| 35-M | Anyone can talk about changing old ways of acting in relationships. I am actually doing it. | 1 | 2 | 3 | 4 | 5 |

37. Please check the box for the description that best describes where you think you are, today, in your efforts to change the way you behave with your partner(s). (Check only one box)

[ ]   I am not really making any changes
[ ]   I am thinking about making changes in the future
[ ]   I am getting ready to make changes or I have made some changes already
[ ]   I have made some important changes and I have more to do
[ ]   I have made the changes I needed to make and now I have to keep up the good work

SAFE AT HOME SCORE SHEET

NOTE: Reverse code each score before totaling and averaging

(1=5, 2=4, 3=3, 4=2, 5=1)

P = Precontemplation **C** = Contemplation **P/A** = Preparation/Action **M** = Maintenance

Reverse ↓	Reverse ↓	Reverse ↓	Reverse ↓
Item # 5 Score ___	Item # 1 Score ___	Item # 3 Score ___	Item # 2 Score ___
Item # 11 Score ___	Item # 4 Score ___	Item # 6 Score ___	Item # 16 Score ___
Item # 14 Score ___	Item # 9 Score ___	Item # 12 Score ___	Item # 19 Score ___
Item # 18 Score ___	Item #10 Score ___	Item # 15 Score ___	Item # 24 Score ___
Item # 20 Score ___	Item #13 Score ___	Item # 22 Score ___	Item # 25 Score ___
Item # 26 Score ___	Item #17 Score ___	Item # 28 Score ___	Item # 33 Score ___
Item # 29 Score ___	Item #21 Score ___	Item # 30 Score ___	Item # 35 Score ___
Item # 34 Score ___	Item #23 Score ___		
	Item #32 Score ___		

Total: _____ Total: _____ Total: _____ Total: _____
/8 = ___.___   /9 = ___.___   /7 = ___.___   /7 = ___.___
(P Average)   (C Average)   (P/A Average)   (M Average)

Pre-contemplation Stage (**P**): Client denies or minimizes having an anger/aggression problem and has no intention in changing
Contemplation Stage (**C**): Client is thinking about changing but has no specific plans
Preparation Stage (**P/A**): Client is preparing for change, or actually implementing a change strategy
Maintenance (**M**): Client is sustaining the changes previously made

Overall Readiness to Change: (C_____ + P/A_____) – P _____ =

_____ (OVERALL Readiness to Change SCORE)

OVERALL Readiness to Change SCORE: Male Average = **5.30** Female Average = **5.63**

For more information: Sielski, C., Begun, A., & Hamel, J. (2015). Expanding knowledge concerning the Safe at Home instruments for assessing readiness-to-change among individuals in batterer treatment. Partner Abuse, 6(3).

THE FIVE STAGES OF CHANGE

Handout

Researchers have found that anyone who makes a successful decision to change something that is not working in his or her life goes through a series of stages. This is true for smoking, dieting, drugs and alcohol, gambling, aggressive behavior, etc.

Everybody who comes into our program enters at their own stage of change. It helps us and it will help you to understand what stage you're at—and to notice at various points in your program if there have been any changes.

If you do notice movement in these stages, it is valuable to figure out how that happened. Usually something "clicks"—or the problems reach a breaking point and you decide you really have to move forward.

Here are the classic stages—maybe you can identify even more:

#1: PRECONTEMPLATION

I don't have a problem with aggression—so I have no interest in changing my behavior.

#2: CONTEMPLATION

I realize I might have a problem with aggression—but I'm not sure I want to do anything about it yet. Maybe later.

#3: PREPARATION (or DETERMINATION)

I know now that I have a problem with aggression—and I have to do something about this so I can have a better life and better relationships.

#4: ACTION

I realize now that my abusive behavior is unacceptable, and I will not allow myself to return to it. I am committing myself to groups, therapy, spiritual guidance, books, and good people—anything to help me make these changes.

#5: MAINTENANCE

I realize that it's going to take a lot of work, over a long period of time, to maintain these changes and keep growing. I have to surround myself with the right people and watch carefully for warning signs that I might be slipping.

MAY NOT BE REPRODUCED WITHOUT PERMISSION

MAKING CHANGES, PROS AND CONS

Handout

Whenever we think about keeping an old behavior or changing it, it helps to weight the pros and cons—then come to an intelligent decision. Try this with your anger/aggression.

GOOD Things About Anger/Aggression	GOOD Things About Changing Anger/Aggression
NOT-GOOD Things About Anger/Aggression	NOT-GOOD Things About Changing Anger/Aggression

MAY NOT BE REPRODUCED WITHOUT PERMISSION

HOMEWORK

Handout

If you did not do this exercise in the group session, fill in the blanks on this chart about the pros and cons of any angry/aggressive behavior.

If you did this in the group, choose different behavior and apply the model to it.

Whenever we think about keeping an old behavior or changing it, it helps to weigh the pros and cons—then come to an intelligent decision. Try this with your anger/aggression.

GOOD Things About Anger/Aggression	GOOD Things About Changing Anger/Aggression
NOT-GOOD Things About Anger/Aggression	NOT-GOOD Things About Changing Anger/Aggression

PREVENTION PLAN*

♦♦♦ **Handout**

Purpose: To prepare you for future situations when you might be tempted to become abusive with your partner.

STEP #2: Cue or Trigger (What could set you off?)

STEP #3: Coping Strategies

1. **SCARE YOURSELF IMAGE—Example**: Remember the damage to your family, remember being arrested, etc. What scary image would have an impact on you?

2. **SELF-TALK—Example:** "This isn't worth it," "Nobody's perfect," "I want to keep my life together." What would that be for you?

3. **RELAXATION/DISTRACTION—Examples:** Deep breathing, listening to music, playing basketball, etc. What would work for you?

4. **FRIENDS/ALLIES—Example:** Call a friend, crisis line, therapist, sponsor, or family member. Who would that be for you?

STEP #1: Behavior I Do NOT Want to Do (be specific)

_____

_____

*Adapted with permission from Wexler, 1991.

HOMEWORK

Handout

Identify three trigger situations that you know could put you at risk for behaving abusively with your partner or kids. Be as specific as possible:

1.

2.

3.

PART V
EXIT/RELAPSE PREVENTION SESSIONS

EXIT SESSION I

Handout

MOST VIOLENT AND/OR MOST DISTURBING INCIDENT

THIS MATERIAL (AND THE MATERIAL FROM EXIT SESSION II) SHOULD BE PRESENTED ONLY WHEN AT LEAST ONE GROUP MEMBER IS NEAR THE END POINT OF THE TREATMENT PROGRAM. THEN THE REGULARLY SCHEDULED GROUP CONTENT SHOULD RESUME.

Program

Here are the suggested instructions for this very important exercise for a group member who is close to terminating the group program:

> *Tell us, in detail, the most disturbing abusive incident that you have committed in your relationship. This is not necessarily the most physically injurious event or the one you got busted for, but rather the one that stands out as the most emotionally upsetting.*

> *There may have been other more abusive incidents in your relationship that were committed by your partner—but the assignment is to look at a situation when YOU have behaved the most abusively toward her.*

> *It is very important for you to describe this incident as vividly as possible, in detail, as if it were happening in slow motion. Each step of the way, we need to hear about your self-talk, your emotions, and your physical state.*

(Note to the group leader: Particularly important is his affect. You may need to say repeatedly, *"Describe how you are feeling at this point."* The goal here is to diminish as much of the original denial and minimization as possible.)

> *We think you're ready for this now in ways that you were not when you first came into this program. This is an opportunity to go into more depth with these issues—particularly with some of the new skills and information that you now have.*

> *We also want you to identify your partner's and child's self-talk, your partner's and child's emotions, and your partner's and child's physical states.*

> *We know you can do this.*

EXIT SESSION II

◆◆◆ Handout

PREVENTION PLAN

The other Exit/Relapse Prevention Session is the *Prevention Plan.* The instructions for this plan are reviewed as a group in Session 26. So, if a group member developed this plan and reviewed it with the group within a few weeks of his graduation from the group, it is not necessary to repeat.

However (since these are almost always open-ended groups), it is quite likely that the group review of Prevention Plans took place early in a group member's cycle of group sessions. If so, he needs to prepare his personalized Prevention Plan and present it to the group as he nears graduation (four weeks or fewer to go).

PART VI
STANDARD FORMS

WEEKLY CHECK-IN

Handout

Name _____ Date _____

1. **SUCCESS.** Describe one way in the past week in which you successfully kept yourself from being aggressive or successfully used something you learned in group. The success can be large or small. This is a chance to pat yourself on the back.

   What was the situation?

   What might you have done in the past?

   What did you do right?

Calmly stood up for my rights		Told myself to relax		Took a Time-Out	
Expressed my feelings responsibly		Changed my self-talk		Other	

2. **SUBSTANCE USE.** Please remember that the first question the court, probation officer, or other referring agency will ask when they learn that you have used is "Was the treatment provider aware of this?" If we were aware of it, we can tell them, "Yes, and here is what we're doing to help him or her." Over the course of the last week, did you use any of the following?

   Alcohol (only report if you are prohibited from drinking as part of your probation mandate)
   Methamphetamine
   Cocaine

   If you answered "yes" to any of the above, please describe the circumstances and the thought the self-talk you used to justify your using.

MAY NOT BE REPRODUCED WITHOUT PERMISSION

3. **PROBLEM SITUATION.** Describe one way in the past week in which you did not handle an interpersonal situation well.

    What was the situation?

    How upset did you feel?

    | 1 | 10 | 20 | 30 | 40 | 50 | 60 | 70 | 80 | 90 | 100 |

    Not At All Upset   Upset   Extremely Upset

    How did you respond?

4. **AGGRESSION.** Did you become verbally or physically aggressive toward anyone in the past week (including threats and damage to property)?

Slapping		Kicking		Grabbing/restraining	
Punching/hitting		Property destruction		Throwing things	
Verbal/emotional abuse		Sexual abuse		Other	

    What would you do in a similar situation in the future to avoid becoming aggressive?

5. **HOMEWORK.** Did you complete homework for the week?

    Yes _____

    No _____

    None Assigned _____

THIS FORM **MAY** BE DUPLICATED FOR USE IN STOP PROGRAM GROUPS

EVALUATION FORM

◆◆◆ **Handout**

This form is to be completed at the end of the group member's 13th, 26th, 39th, and 52nd sessions (for a 52-week program), as well as at any other time when there are special recommendations or concerns.

Group Member's Name: _____

Group Leaders' Names: _____

_____

Group Attended: _____ Dates: _____ to _____

Total # sessions attended: _____ Date of report: _____

Please evaluate the group member on all the scales listed below. The norm group should be the overall population of group members at this stage of treatment. Give a "1" for the lowest score on each item and a "9" for the highest score, with any number in between that best describes your assessment.

PARTICIPATION

No personal self-disclosure	1 2 3 4 5 6 7 8 9	Appropriate self-disclosure
Defensive	1 2 3 4 5 6 7 8 9	Very open to feedback
Feedback aggressive/destructive	1 2 3 4 5 6 7 8 9	Feedback constructive
Does not complete homework	1 2 3 4 5 6 7 8 9	Completes homework

BEHAVIOR

Poor ability expressing feelings	1 2 3 4 5 6 7 8 9	Excellent ability
Does not recognize responsibility for family violence	1 2 3 4 5 6 7 8 9	Recognizes responsibility
Poor control over impulses and behavior	1 2 3 4 5 6 7 8 9	Good control
Minimal empathy/concern for victim or other family members	1 2 3 4 5 6 7 8 9	Excellent empathy/concern
Little self-awareness of buildup of tension or emotional needs	1 2 3 4 5 6 7 8 9	Excellent self-awareness
Poor assertive expression of needs and feelings	1 2 3 4 5 6 7 8 9	Excellent assertiveness

Please rate the group member's overall progress, **as compared to the overall population of group members at this stage of treatment**. Rate on a scale of 1 to 9, with 1 as no improvement and 9 as outstanding improvement.

1   2   3   4   5   6   7   8   9   N/A

At this time, check the box if you recommend either of the following:

Probation_____

Termination from program_____

COMMENTS

_____

_____

_____

_____

_____

Group leader signature _____

Group leader signature _____

TREATMENT EXPECTATIONS

Handout

Here are some basic guidelines about what treatment programs typically expect from group members at various stages of their treatment. These expectations are based on a 52-week program and may be adapted, depending on the length of treatment.

Treatment Expectations for Weeks 1–12

1. PARTICIPATION: Arrives on time, is attentive, asks questions, contributes constructively to group discussions, is able to describe incident that brought him or her to program
2. ATTITUDE: Uses respectful language, demonstrates gender respect, demonstrates respect for group process and other members, accepts accountability for actions
3. HOMEWORK: Completes assignments, shows thought and effort
4. BASIC SKILLS: Uses "I statements," reports appropriate use of Time-Outs, identifies red flags, uses listening skills

Treatment Expectations for Weeks 13–25

1. PARTICIPATION: Arrives on time, is attentive, asks questions, contributes constructively to group discussions, voluntarily participates
2. ATTITUDE: Uses respectful language, demonstrates gender respect, demonstrates respect for group process and other members, accepts accountability for actions
3. HOMEWORK: Completes assignments, shows thought and effort
4. BASIC SKILLS: Uses "I statements," reports appropriate use of Time-Outs, identifies red flags, uses listening skills
5. ADVANCED SKILLS: Exhibits reflective listening, utilizes compromise and negotiation tools, identifies personal strengths and weaknesses (positive change and areas of concern), uses noncontrolling communication

Treatment Expectations for Weeks 26–39

1. PARTICIPATION: Arrives on time, is attentive, asks questions, contributes constructively to group discussions, voluntarily participates, initiates constructive dialogue, appropriately challenges others
2. ATTITUDE: Uses respectful language, demonstrates gender respect, demonstrates respect for group process and other members, accepts accountability for actions, consistently models positive changes in behavior and attitude
3. HOMEWORK: Completes assignments, shows better developed thought and effort
4. BASIC SKILLS: Consistently uses "I statements," reports appropriate use of Time-Outs, identifies red flags, uses listening skills

MAY NOT BE REPRODUCED WITHOUT PERMISSION

5. ADVANCED SKILLS: Consistently uses and models: reflective listening, utilizing compromise and negotiation tools, identifying personal strengths and weaknesses (positive change and areas of concern), using noncontrolling communication; reports use of new skills in current relationships

Treatment Expectations for Weeks 40–52

1. PARTICIPATION: Arrives on time, is consistently attentive, asks questions, contributes constructively to group discussions, voluntarily participates, initiates constructive dialogue, appropriately challenges others

2. ATTITUDE: Uses respectful language, demonstrates gender respect, demonstrates respect for group process and other members, accepts accountability for actions, consistently models positive changes in behavior and attitude, maintains self-confidence and commitment to nonviolence

3. HOMEWORK: Completes assignments, shows better developed thought and effort, generates approved relapse prevention plan

4. BASIC SKILLS: Consistently uses "I statements," reports appropriate use of Time-Outs, identifies red flags, uses listening skills

5. ADVANCED SKILLS: Consistently uses and models: reflective listening, compromise and negotiation tools, identification of personal strengths and weaknesses (positive change and areas of concern), noncontrolling communication; provides positive modeling for other group members; demonstrates empathy for victim, children, and others

THE STOP PROGRAM

FOR WOMEN

2nd EDITION

HANDOUTS AND HOMEWORK

INNOVATIVE

SKILLS, **T**ECHNIQUES, **O**PTIONS, AND **P**LANS

FOR BETTER RELATIONSHIPS

These handouts provide the information and "homework" that will keep your program participants actively engaged in overcoming their abuse tendencies. Packaged for optimum flexibility, handouts can be added, removed, or rearranged, allowing you to modify the program so that it best suits your needs. *The STOP Program* handouts are copyrighted, however, and may not be reproduced. To order additional copies of the handouts please visit www.wwnorton.com or call 1-800-233-4830.

DAVID B. WEXLER

Contents

Welcome! 1

Part I: Orientation Information

The STOP Program for Women Q&A 3
Typical Questions and Concerns 6
Provisional Status Policy (Group Members' Version) 7
The Fifteen Commandments of STOP 8
Weekly Check-In 9
Gut Check Questionnaire 11
Evaluation Form 12
Gratitude Statements 14
One-Minute Mindfulness in Everyday Life 15
Feelings Count 16

Part II: New Member Sessions

House of Abuse 18
Time-Out 19
Time-Out Information for Partners 21

Part III: Core Curriculum

Female Abuse Wheel 22
Red Flags of Anger 23
Session 1 Homework #1 24
Session 1 Homework #2 25
What's Your Anger Style? 27
The Four-Square Technique 29
Healthy Anger/Destructive Aggression 30
Letting Go of Anger 32
Session 2 Homework 33
Put-Downs From Parents 34
Forgiving the Self 35
Session 3 Homework 36
Adverse Childhood Experiences (ACE) Info 37
What's My ACE Score? 39
Session 4 Homework 43
ACE Resilience Questionnaire 45
Thinking the Worst 47
The Stories of Trauma 48
Session 5 Homework 49

Girlfriends and Social Support 50
The House of Self-Worth and Empowerment 51
Session 6 Homework 52
Bad Rap 54
Bad Rap Quiz 55
Stories We Tell Ourselves 56
Session 7 Homework 57
Jealousy: Taming the Green-Eyed Monster 58
Stories of Jealousy: I Knew I Was Right 60
Session 8 Homework 61
Switch! 62
Session 9 Homework 63
Assertiveness 64
What Is Assertive Behavior? 65
Boundary Violations 66
Session 10 Homework 67
Respectful Feedback 68
Asking for Change 69
How We Talk Ourselves Out of It 70
Session 11 Homework 71
Active Listening 72
Communication Roadblocks 74
Session 12 Homework #1 75
Session 12 Homework #2 76
The Five Love Languages 77
Session 13 Homework 79
Four Horsemen of the Apocalypse 80
Emotional Abuse and Mind Games 81
Conflict With Respect 82
Session 14 Homework 84
The Art of Apologies 85
Classic Apology Mistakes 87
Session 15 Homework #1 88
Session 15 Homework #2 89
Can I Count On You? 93
Secure Communication 94
Session 16 Homework 95
Relationship Respect Contract 99
Contract Violations 100
Session 17 Homework 101
Why Men Keep Their Mouths Shut About Domestic Violence 103
Session 18 Homework 104
Sexual Put-Downs and Mind Games 105
About Sex 106
Session 19 Homework 107
Who Decides? 108
Rules and Roles: Spoken and Unspoken 110
Session 20 Homework 111
Questions for Kids 112
Session 21 Homework 113
Accountability Assumption 114

Accountability Defenses 115
Accountability Statement 116
Session 22 Homework #1 117
Session 22 Homework #2 118
I Really Didn't Mean To Do It... I Was Drunk 121
Why Do We Care? The Relationship Between Substance Abuse and Intimate Partner Violence 122
Why Do I Use? 123
Session 23 Homework 124
Stake in Conformity 125
Screw You! 126
Session 24 Homework #1 127
Session 24 Homework #2 128
The Five Stages of Change 133
Making Changes, Pros and Cons 134
Session 25 Homework 135
The Prevention Plan 136
Session 26 Homework 137

WELCOME!

Welcome to the STOP Program for Women. You are here because of a report indicating that you were involved in an incident of relationship violence. This destructive behavior has damaged other people close to you (emotionally and/or physically)—and it has been damaging to you as well. Even though your partner or other people in your life may have acted destructively as well, our focus in this program is on the one person over whom you have control: yourself.

This program will help you discover how abusive patterns in your most intimate relationships began—and it will help you develop new ways of dealing with the beliefs and emotions that have triggered these behaviors.

The same relationship issues can emerge in straight and LGBTQ+ relationships—and the STOP Program for Women group leaders are trained to understand and help with all types of intimate partner relationships. Many of the handouts use examples of situations for female same-sex couples.

The STOP Program for Women should really be called the "GO Program"—because it is designed to move forward with something better and new, not just stop the destructive and old.

Some of the issues are difficult to face, but the STOP Program for Women will help you deal with these problems in a supportive learning environment.

The STOP Program for Women offers women (just like the men in men's groups) intensive training in new skills for self-management, communication, problem solving, and empathy for others. Special attention is paid to the self-talk that determine emotions and behaviors in any given situation.

And this program especially helps women examine the ways they have been victimized in their personal lives—WITHOUT allowing these victim experiences to be used as an excuse for aggressive or abusive behavior.

But, most importantly, the STOP Program for Women group leaders consistently use an approach that emphasizes respect for women's experiences—both in personal history and in present relationships. The group leaders will always try to be compassionate and understanding about why you choose to act the way you do.

In a series of weekly groups, you and the other women in your group will have a chance to discuss family problems, feelings that led to destructive behaviors, and the impact violence has had on your relationships. We strongly emphasize new ways of communicating, handling stress, and resolving conflicts. Each session is designed to focus on a particular aspect of family violence. At each session your group leaders will assign exercises, handouts, and homework, which are included here.

This model has been carefully constructed through decades of trial and error with thousands of women and through paying attention to new research in the field. We would like to thank all the women who have given so much of themselves and worked so hard throughout the years during which we have been developing the program. We have found that domestic violence has many causes and consequences and that each man and woman has a unique story to tell.

Although many of the group sessions involve learning specific skills such as stress management and improved communication, the groups are considered to be group counseling. This means that we encourage you to think about your own life, discuss your feelings, and offer support for other group members. You will get from this program what you put into it. Use your time well.

PART I
ORIENTATION INFORMATION

THE STOP PROGRAM FOR WOMEN Q&A

Welcome to the STOP Program for Women. The following is a list of answers to frequently asked questions about the groups. Please read this information carefully.

1. *Why was I referred to the STOP Program for Women?*
   You were referred to this program because of reports that you were involved in one or more incidents of relationship violence. The fact that you have been referred to the STOP Program for Women indicates that this problem is treatable.

2. *How often do the groups meet?*
   Each group meets for two hours, once each week.

3. *Who else is in the group?*
   The group members include women like yourself who have been involved in some sort of relationship violence. This is an ongoing group. It is very valuable to have group members at different stages of treatment to help explain to you how the group works. The group may include women in both straight and gay relationships.

4. *What happens in the group?*
   Our philosophy is that women who get into trouble in their relationships need to learn new skills. We want to make sure that you have new ways of handling stress, new ways of thinking about difficult relationship situations, and new ways of problem solving. When you leave this program, you should have lots of new tools to help you handle things differently. This will make it much less likely that the same problems will take place.

   Each session is designed to focus on a particular aspect of relationship health and/or relationship violence. Groups provide an atmosphere to discuss the problems, feelings that have led to destructive behavior, and the impact violence has had on the relationship. New ways of understanding yourself, understanding others, and relating to other people are strongly emphasized.

5. *Is this a class or group counseling?*
   Although many of the group sessions may involve teaching of specific skills, such as stress management and improved communication, the groups are considered to be group counseling. This means that a strong emphasis is placed on self-examination,

discussion of feelings, and support for other group members. Most people benefit from the group based on how committed they are to engage in these tasks.

6. *Do I have to come every week?*
You are required to attend every week. Research indicates that there is a direct relationship between steady attendance and treatment progress. In order for you to benefit from the program, attendance must become a priority. As you become more involved in the group, you will probably find out that you are motivated to attend, not only for your own benefit, but also to support your fellow group members.

7. *What about absences?*
We recognize that there may be circumstances which require you to miss a group session. If you are unable to attend a group session, please notify our staff beforehand to let us know that you will be unable to attend. Documentation of all absences is required and should be given to our staff prior to your absence. If you miss a group for unexpected reasons, please bring in documentation for the absence at the next group session. Undocumented absences will be considered unexcused.

Unexcused absences indicate a lack of interest or commitment to change your situation. An unexcused absence will be grounds for a report back to your probation officer or other referring agency, which may result in the termination of treatment.

8. *What happens if I arrive late?*
If a group member arrives more than five minutes late, she will be marked as late. Three times late will be treated as the equivalent of one unexcused absence. If a group member arrives 15 or more minutes late, she will under no circumstances be allowed into the group, and this will be considered an unexcused absence.

9. *Who leads the group?*
All of the group leaders are certified domestic violence counselors who have had extensive training in the treatment of relationship violence.

10. *Are there additional expectations for successful participation other than group attendance?*
All sessions have homework assignments that you will be expected to complete and bring to the next group meeting. The group leaders will review the homework assignment with you at the end of each group meeting so you will know what is expected. The group leaders will also discuss the completed homework at the beginning of each group meeting. Three missed homework assignments will be considered the equivalent of one unexcused absence. This will be grounds for a report back to your probation officer, case manager, social worker, or other referring agency, which may result in the termination of treatment.

Group members are required to be at the site 10 minutes before the starting time for the group in order to fill out a questionnaire titled "Weekly Check-In." Group will not begin until everyone completes the questionnaire.

You will be given a STOP Program for Women: Homework and Handouts binder at the first group meeting. Each week, information from the binder will be discussed during the group session. You are expected to bring your binder to each group meeting.

11. *What about confidentiality? Can what I say in the group be used against me?*
    Since this treatment uses a team approach, you can assume that what you say in the group may be discussed with your probation officer, case manager, social worker, or other referring agency. Only information that is directly related to your treatment goals is included in these reports. Most of the personal issues and feelings discussed in the group sessions remain confidential.

    In certain situations, the group leaders are obligated to report information that is revealed in the group. These reportable situations include serious threats of hurting or killing someone else, serious threats of hurting or killing yourself, new and significant reports of family violence (including incidents in which children have suffered emotional damage from witnessing spousal abuse), child abuse, or elder abuse.

12. *What about new incidents of violence in my relationship?*
    As a participant in domestic violence treatment, you are expected to discuss any new incidents of violence in your relationships. Presenting information about new incidents of violence does not necessarily lead to termination if you are genuinely remorseful, take responsibility for your actions, and appear to be making efforts to prevent a similar reoccurrence in the future. Keep in mind that it is in your best interest to disclose a new incident of violence. When these incidents are discovered through other sources, it impacts negatively on you.

13. *What about electronic devices?*
    During the group session, please turn off all electronic devices. You will have an opportunity during the break to return phone messages.

14. *How should I dress for the group?*
    There is no specific dress code for these sessions.

15. *Any other rules about appropriate behavior?*
    While on the premises of this agency, you are asked to use respectful language that is not offensive to staff or other clients being served.
    No use of alcohol or illegal drugs prior to the group session.
    Group members will not threaten or intimidate other group members or leaders at any time.
    I have read the above information and agree to the conditions of treatment.

_____   _____
Group Member's Signature   Print Name

_____   _____
Date   Group Name

TYPICAL QUESTIONS AND CONCERNS

1. *Won't group counseling try and get me to let out all my emotions? I'm not comfortable with that!*
   Everybody in group counseling is different, and each person decides how much of her personal emotions and personal experiences to reveal to others. No one is expected to walk right in and talk about their deepest feelings in front of a bunch of strangers.

   Over time, most people become more and more comfortable letting the group know more about what is happening inside. We know that there is usually a correlation between talking about yourself and getting some benefit from the sessions. But this all happens at the pace of the individual.

2. *I would rather have individual counseling because I don't like talking in front of other people and I can get more personal attention.*
   The STOP Program philosophy is that these kinds of problems are best treated in a group setting. You get the benefit of hearing about the experiences of others and learning from their successes and mistakes. The feedback from peers is one of the single most important factors in predicting positive outcome.

3. *I don't want to be in a group with a bunch of violent and abusive women—I'm not like them!*
   We treat the woman, not the label. We stay away from labels that sound like put-downs. Instead, we focus on the specific thoughts, feelings, and situations that have led to problem behaviors. We could put any woman in this group, regardless of what has gone wrong in her behavior with others, and she would benefit from the approaches used in this treatment model.

PROVISIONAL STATUS POLICY (GROUP MEMBERS' VERSION)

The following are grounds for group members to be placed on Provisional Status in the STOP Program for Women (leading to possible termination). These behaviors are in addition to activity that takes place outside of the group sessions, such as acts of violence, repeated drug or alcohol problems, or failure to attend group:

1. **Consistently** putting down men or minimizing violence
2. **Persistent** disruptive or oppositional behavior in group
3. **Consistent** projection of blame for relationship problems without self-examination
4. **Consistent** lack of participation in group, including failure to complete homework assignments
5. **Consistent** pattern of telling stories (bragging or showing off) about controlling, abusive, or violent behavior with little or no signs of remorse

THE FIFTEEN COMMANDMENTS OF STOP

1. We are all 100% responsible for our own actions. Even when it *feels* like someone else made us do it.
2. Violence is not an acceptable solution to problems.
3. Anger is normal. Being consumed by anger, or being driven to commit acts of aggression or retaliation because of anger, is not.
4. Recognize that anger is—always—a secondary emotion. Identify the primary one first, and you are really in a position of power.
5. We do not have control over any other person, but we do have control over ourselves.
6. We can always take a time-out before reacting.
7. We can't do anything about the past, but we can change the future.
8. Self-talk is everything. We are always telling ourselves stories about the events in our world—and the stories can always change.
9. Sometimes anger can be very quiet and cold. Just because you are not yelling—or even if you are smiling—does not mean that you are not being aggressive.
10. Just because it feels like someone deserves retaliation doesn't mean it is wise, productive, or moral to deliver it.
11. When you let go of anger, you are doing yourself a big favor. You are no longer allowing the situation or the person to control you.
12. Use gratitudes when you need to, and appreciate the power and positivity they will confer on you.
13. Always have a Prevention Plan in your back pocket. And think of the big picture (the "other three squares").
14. Although there are differences between men and women, our needs and rights are fundamentally alike.
15. Counselors and case managers cannot make people change—they can only set the stage for change to occur.

THE STOP PROGRAM FOR WOMEN: WEEKLY CHECK-IN

◆ Handout

Name _____ Date _____

1. **SUCCESS.** Describe one way in the past week in which you successfully kept yourself from being aggressive or successfully used something you learned in group. The success can be large or small. This is a chance to pat yourself on the back.

   What was the situation?

   What might you have done in the past?

   What did you do right?

Calmly stood up for my rights		Told myself to relax		Took a Time-Out	
Expressed my feelings responsibly		Changed my self-talk		Other	

2. **SUBSTANCE USE.** Please remember that the first question the court, probation officer, or other referring agency will ask, when they receive knowledge that you have used, is: "Was the treatment provider aware of this?" If we were aware of it, we can tell them, "Yes, and here is what we're doing to help him or her." Over the course of the last week did you use any of the following?

Alcohol (only report if you are prohibited from drinking as part of your probation mandate)		Methamphetamine		Cocaine	

If you answered *yes* to any of the above, please describe the circumstances, and the thought you used that gave you permission. _____

_____

_____

_____

3. **PROBLEM SITUATION.** Describe one way in the past week in which you did not handle an interpersonal situation well.

   What was the situation?

   How upset did you feel?

0	10	20	30	40	50	60	70	80	90	100
Not at All Upset					Upset					Extremely Upset

   How did you respond?

4. **AGGRESSION.** Did you become verbally or physically aggressive toward anyone in the past week (including threats and damage to property)?

Slapping		Kicking		Grabbing/Restraining	
Punching/Hitting		Property Destruction		Throwing Things	
Verbal/Emotional Abuse		Sexual Abuse		Other	

   What would you do in a similar situation in the future to avoid becoming aggressive?

5. **HOMEWORK.** Did you complete homework for the week?

   Yes _____   No _____   None Assigned _____

PLEASE NOTE:
YOU HAVE FULL PERMISSION TO COPY THIS FORM FOR GROUP USE.

GUT CHECK QUESTIONNAIRE

◆ Handout

Adapted with permission from Dutton, D. G. (1998). The abusive personality: Violence and control in intimate relationships. New York: Guilford Press.

Name _____ Date _____

Answer each of these questions as honestly as you can. None of these answers will be shared with the group without your consent. Use a number from 1 to 10, with 1 being lowest and 10 being highest. When answering questions 4, 5, and 6, remember that the purpose of this is simply to offer some valuable feedback to one of your peers. Most of us have trouble seeing ourselves clearly without honest feedback from others who care about us.

1. How honest am I being in the group? *(Not at all/Completely)* _____ (1-10)

2. How much effort am I putting into the group? *(Not at all/Completely)* _____ (1-10)

3. How much feedback am I giving to others in the group? *(Not at all/Completely)* _____ (1-10)

4. Who do I know the most/least in the group?

    Most _____

    Least _____

5. Who is acknowledging responsibility for her relationship problems most in the group?

    Most _____

6. Who is being the most emotionally honest in the group?

    Most _____

7. How much am I getting out of the group?

1	2	3	4	5	6	7	8	9	10
Nothing		A little		Some value			A lot		Very much

STOP PROGRAM: EVALUATION FORM

◆ Handout

This sample form is to be completed at the end of sessions 13, 26, 39, and 52 (for a 52-week program), as well as any other time when there are special recommendations or concerns.

Group member's name: _____

Group leaders' names: _____

_____

Group attended: _____ Dates: _____ to _____

Total # sessions attended: _____ Date of report: _____

Please evaluate the group member on all the scales listed below. The norm group should be the overall population of group members at this stage of treatment. Give a 1 for the lowest score on each item and a 9 for the highest score, with any number in between that best describes your assessment.

PARTICIPATION

No personal self-disclosure	1 2 3 4 5 6 7 8 9	Appropriate self-disclosure
Defensive	1 2 3 4 5 6 7 8 9	Very open to feedback
Feedback aggressive/destructive	1 2 3 4 5 6 7 8 9	Feedback constructive
Does not complete homework	1 2 3 4 5 6 7 8 9	Completes homework

BEHAVIOR

Poor ability expressing feelings	1 2 3 4 5 6 7 8 9	Excellent ability
Does not recognize responsibility for family violence	1 2 3 4 5 6 7 8 9	Recognizes responsibility
Poor control over impulses and behavior	1 2 3 4 5 6 7 8 9	Good control
Minimal empathy/concern for victim or other family members	1 2 3 4 5 6 7 8 9	Excellent empathy/concern
Little self-awareness of buildup of tension or emotional needs	1 2 3 4 5 6 7 8 9	Excellent self-awareness
Poor assertive expression of needs and feelings	1 2 3 4 5 6 7 8 9	Excellent assertiveness

EVALUATION FORM – PAGE 2

◆ **Handout**

Please rate the group member's overall progress, **as compared to the overall population of group members at this stage of treatment.** Rate on a scale of 1-9, with 1 as no improvement and 9 as outstanding improvement.

   1   2   3   4   5   6   7   8   9   N/A

At this time, check the box if you recommend either of the following:

Probation: _____

Termination from program: _____

COMMENTS

_____

_____

_____

_____

_____

_____

_____

Group leader signature _____

Group leader signature _____

GRATITUDE STATEMENTS

- Does gratitude really affect your brain at the biological level? YES!
- The antidepressant Wellbutrin boosts the neurotransmitter called dopamine. So does gratitude.
- Prozac boosts the neurotransmitter called *serotonin*. So does gratitude.
- It's not finding gratitude that matters most; it's remembering to look in the first place. Remembering to be grateful is a form of emotional intelligence.
- And gratitude doesn't just make your brain happy—it can also create a positive feedback loop in your relationships. So express that gratitude to the people you care about.

It's not happiness that brings us gratitude. It's gratitude that bring us happiness.
People who kept a list of a few things they were grateful for each day . . .

- exercise more/feel more energy and vitality
- are less bothered by pain
- sleep 30 minutes more each night
- feel closer and more connected to others
- report greater well-being and optimism
- report more attentiveness, enthusiasm, and determination
- cope better with situations that might have made them angry

For example, it can be very valuable to think of one person who has been very important to you, and write down the three most important things that this person has done for you.

At the beginning of each session, we will ask you to share some "good stuff" that you have noticed since we last met. Here are examples of things that might happen in your life in a typical week that are worthy of gratitude:

- *I had a great conversation with my partner last night—I used what we learned in the group, and he said it was one of the best conversations we ever had. I am so grateful.*
- *I talked to a friend of mine and helped her out with a problem. I am grateful that I got a chance to do that.*
- *Somebody at work here really took one of my concerns seriously and followed through on it. I am really grateful.*
- *I watched my kids playing together last night and they were really getting along. I really felt lucky.*

ONE-MINUTE MINDFULNESS IN EVERYDAY LIFE

Mindfulness is a form of self-awareness training: a state of being *in the present* and *accepting things for what they are* (non-judgmentally).

In practice, we want you to just observe whatever happens. Label any thoughts (*oh, there goes a "worried" thought*) and then leave them alone—just be prepared to let them float away. Pay attention to your breathing or simply notice your surroundings instead.

When emotions or memories show up, just give them labels like *that's a sad feeling* or *that's an angry feeling*—and then just allow them to drift away. These memories and feelings will gradually decrease in intensity and frequency.

It is especially helpful to know that you can get a LOT of benefit from mindfulness even if you just practice it for one minute—especially if you can do it several times a day. This is not hard to do, because there is always a minute here or a minute there when you are standing in line, waiting on a phone hold, or just about to walk in the door at home.

One-Minute Mindfulness Technique

In our group, we practice ONE-MINUTE MINDFULNESS every session. Start by sitting in a comfortable and balanced position. Then breathe slowly and deeply several times. Then . . .

- Focus your entire attention on holding a pen or pencil between your fingers for one minute.
- Chew on a raisin for one minute, paying full attention to the taste and texture of this experience.
- Walk three feet (and no more), taking a full minute to take the steps, focusing on all the sensations and feelings in your body as you move so slowly.
- Pick a spot on the wall across from you and focus all of your attention on that spot for one minute.
- Invent your own!

You may be pleasantly surprised to discover what a difference these minutes make. And you can do this anywhere.

FEELINGS COUNT

◆ Handout

Happy And Confident

Accepted	Alive	Brave	Calm	Caring	Cheerful
Comfortable	Confident	Excited	Friendly	Fulfilled	Generous
Grateful	Happy	Hopeful	Joyful	Lovable	Loving
Peaceful	Playful	Powerful	Proud	Relaxed	Relieved
Respected	Secure	Understood	Valuable	Warm	Worthwhile

Fearful and Worried

Anxious	Apprehensive	Confused	Desperate	Distrustful
Fearful	Helpless	Horrified	Inhibited	Out of Control
Trapped	Panicky	Pressured	Threatened	Overwhelmed
Troubled	Uncertain	Uneasy	Uptight	Vulnerable
Worried				

Angry And Resentful

Angry	Bitter	Contemptuous	Disgusted	Disrespected
Frustrated	Furious	Hostile	Impatient	Irritated
Outraged	Provoked	Resentful	Stubborn	Unappreciated
Used	Victimized			

Sad And Pessimistic

Confused	Defeated	Depressed	Devastated	Disappointed
Discouraged	Helpless	Hopeless	Isolated	Lonely
Miserable	Trapped	Sad	Stuck	Overwhelmed
Useless				

Uncomfortable And Insecure

Awkward	Embarrassed	Foolish	Humiliated	Inhibited
Insecure	Self-conscious	Shy	Uncomfortable	

Apologetic And Guilty

Apologetic	Guilty	Remorseful	Sorry	Untrustworthy

Hurt And Rejected

Devastated	Excluded	Hurt	Ignored	Rejected
Vulnerable				

Jealous And Left Out

Envious	Deprived	Left out	Jealous

Ashamed And Inadequate

Ashamed	Inferior	Inadequate	Incompetent	Stupid
Useless	Unattractive	Unworthy	Powerless	

PART II
NEW MEMBER SESSIONS

THE HOUSE OF ABUSE

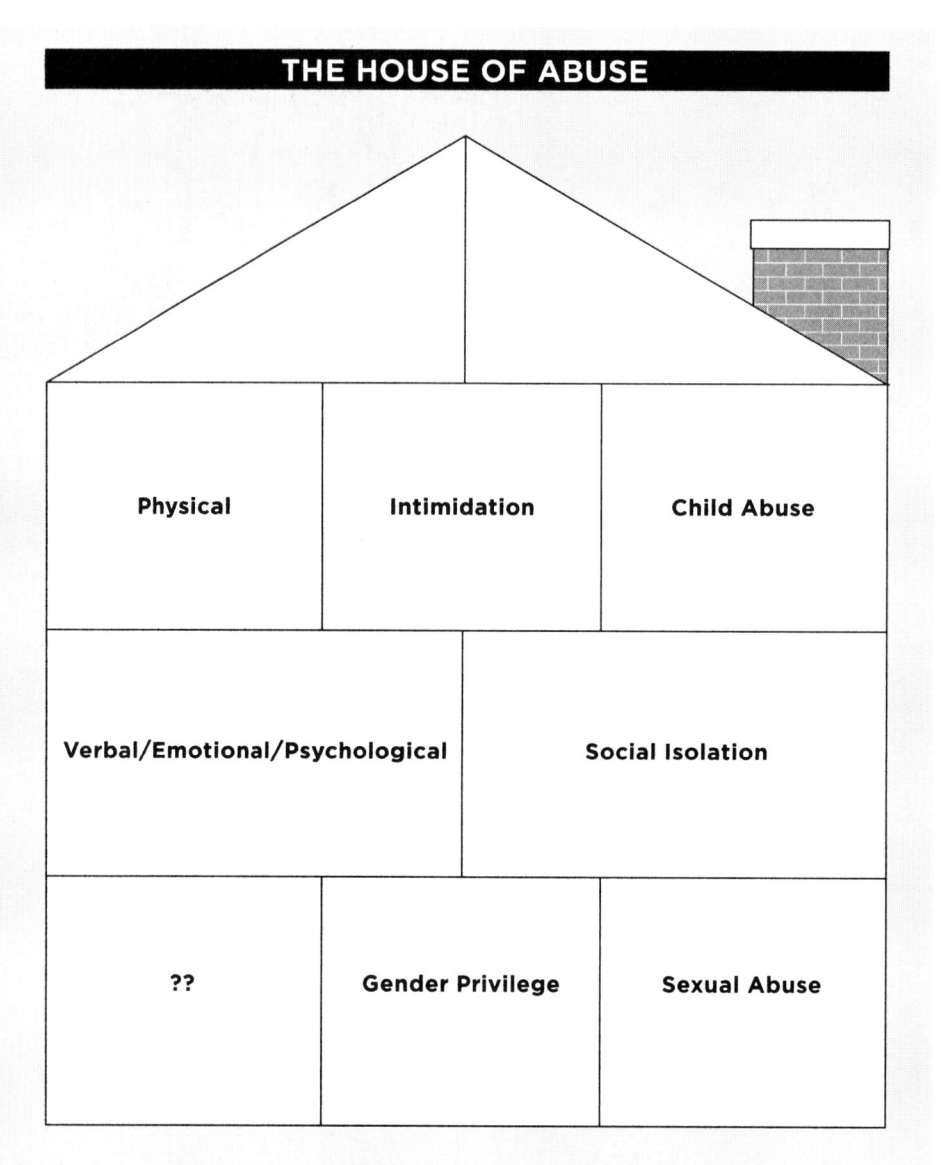

Physical	Intimidation	Child Abuse
Verbal/Emotional/Psychological		Social Isolation
??	Gender Privilege	Sexual Abuse

Adapted with permission from Fischer, K. L., & McGrane, M. F. (1997). *Journey beyond abuse: A step-by-step guide to facilitating women's domestic abuse groups*. St Paul: Amherst H. Wilder Foundation.

TIME-OUT

Handout

The time-out is an emergency strategy to prevent dangerous escalation of conflicts. It should *only* be used in crisis—and as you learn better communication and self-management skills, it may never have to be used at all. But you must know how to use it effectively.

IF YOU USE A TIME-OUT FREQUENTLY, SOMETHING IS SERIOUSLY WRONG WITH YOUR RELATIONSHIP. DO NOT USE TIME-OUT SIMPLY BECAUSE YOU WISH TO AVOID TALKING ABOUT A CERTAIN SUBJECT. THIS IS FOR EMERGENCIES ONLY, AND YOU MUST BE PREPARED TO RESUME THE DISCUSSION LATER ON.

Time-out should not be used as a weapon against the other person. It should not be used as a way of avoiding conflicts. It should not be used as a way of making the other person feel abandoned (*"I'm outta here, dude—I'll show you who's in charge!"*).

Instead, time-out should be used as a sign of respect for the relationship. The message is this: *I care enough about us that I don't want any more damage to this relationship.*
It is essential that your partner understand this message of respect. It is your job to clearly explain this in advance—and to follow it up by your actions when using the time-out correctly.

1. *I'm beginning to feel like things are getting out of control.*
2. *And I don't want to do anything that would mess up our relationship.*
3. *So I need to take a time-out.*
4. *I'm going out for a walk around the neighborhood (or my sister's house, or the gym, etc.).*
5. *I'll be back in (five minutes, or one hour, etc.).*
6. *And let's try talking about this again when I get back. Okay?*

Partner responds:

7. *Okay. Time-out.*

If he or she does not acknowledge, begin the time-out anyway—*without* making any physical contact or threats!

- Leave silently—no door slamming.
- While away, don't drink or use drugs—and don't drive if your temper is out of control.
- Try using self-talk that will help you keep this in perspective:
    - I'm getting upset, but I don't have to lose my cool!
    - I'm frustrated, but I don't have to control anybody else or always get my way.
    - I can calm myself and think through this situation.
    - I've got to think about what will be most important for the future.

- Do something physical (walking, playing sports, working out, etc.) if it will help you discharge tension. Try distracting yourself with any activity that temporarily takes your mind off the intensity of the argument.

- **You must come back when you said you would, or call and check in.** When you come back, decide together if you want to continue the discussion. Here are the options at this point:
    - **Discuss it now:** This is usually the best and most respectful action, but there are some exceptions.
    - **Drop the issue:** Maybe you both realize now that it was really not that big a deal.
    - **Put the issue on hold:** This may be important to discuss, but it would be better to do it at later time. As long as *both* parties agree, this can work.

- Each person has the right to say *no* to further discussion at that time and to suggest a time for discussion. If anger escalates again, take another time-out.

TIME-OUT INFORMATION FOR PARTNERS

Handout

1. **How do time-outs help solve our family problems?**
   Your partner's use of time-outs will prevent both of you from escalating into physical or psychological abuse. Time-outs alone do not solve destructive conflicts, but if used faithfully they will help you both avoid extremely destructive behavior. No respectful communication takes place when there is abuse. Time-outs should be used in an emergency to prevent irreparable damage to the relationship.

2. **What do I do if every time I want to discuss an important topic with my partner, she says she is taking a time-out?**
   Let your partner take the time-out anyway. If she becomes angry and abusive, you will not be able to talk about the problems. At first, she may take time-outs a lot. Just remind yourself that it is only one step and that she will be using other approaches as well.

3. **What if my partner refuses to discuss the matter even after the time-out?**
   Notice on the instruction sheet that she has several choices as to what she does after a time-out. She is not supposed to drop issues if they are important to you. However, she may put them on hold until she is able to both calmly speak and *listen to you*. If she refuses to discuss an issue, your insisting will *not* bring about communication. Let her know that you are still interested in talking about the issue, but be willing to set a later time when she can be calmer while discussing it.

4. **Should I remind my partner to take a time-out when she is getting angry or abusive?**
   No. She is responsible for identifying her own feelings and taking the time-out. As long as you do it for her, she is *not* doing her job. If you are upset about her abuse, you take a time-out for yourself as long as you can do it safely. Remember, you cannot control another person's behavior; you can only protect yourself.

5. **What should I do when she takes a time-out during a discussion?**
   Remind yourself that this is the first step—that it is better for her to take a time-out than to be abusive toward you. Waiting for her to return can lead to your feeling frustrated or abandoned. You can use the time for yourself and then go about your regular business.

6. **Would time-outs be useful for me?**
   Yes. If you find your own anger rising, a time-out is a tool you can use to calm down before you go further in working out a conflict. However, your time-outs will not necessarily change your partner's behaviors.

PART III
CORE CURRICULUM

FEMALE ABUSE WHEEL

Center: FEAR/EXPRESSION/TRAUMA

PHYSICAL
- Hitting/pushing/choking/scratching/pinching
- Biting/kicking/spitting/restraining/slapping/pulling hair
- Hitting with weapons or objects/shooting/stabbing
- Damaging property/pets

THREATS/INTIMIDATION
- To get him fired
- To commit suicide
- To kill him, or to kill or harm his new partner or family
- To file false charges
- To expose him to family, friends, or workplace
- To get him deported or in trouble with the law

VERBAL
- Arguing with him to the point of exhaustion
- Putting him down
- Making him think he's crazy/playing mind-games
- Humiliating him in front of others
- Manipulating him into feeling guilty

FINANCIAL
- Getting credit in his name—then ruining it
- Refusing to contribute income to basic expenses
- Forcing him to take higher-paying, more hazardous, less satisfying job
- Preventing him from getting or keeping a job

HARASSMENT
- Smashing things/destroying his property
- Following him (driving by home/workplace)
- Calling or texting at all hours/calling his home and hanging up
- Posting humiliating details about him on social media

GENDER PRIVILEGE
- Insisting on high level lifestyle
- Refusing to work because men are supposed to support women
- Taunting him by being violent and knowing that nobody will believe him because he's the guy

SEX
- Withholding sex except as a "reward"
- Flirting to make him insecure and jealous
- Purposely getting pregnant without his consent
- Humiliating his body or sexual performance
- Threatening to reveal secrets about his sexuality

USING CHILDREN
- Making him feel guilty about the children
- Using the children to relay messages or spy on him
- Alienating children from him
- Using visitation to harass him
- Threatening to take the children away

Adapted with permission from "Female Aggression Wheel," created by Araceli Cabarcas in Koonin, M., Cabarcas, A., & Geffner, R. (2002). Women Ending Abusive/Violent Episodes Respectfully (WEAVER) Manual. San Diego CA: Family Violence and Sexual Assault Institute.

RED FLAGS OF ANGER

Handout

Red flags are warnings. They tell us that we are entering an emotional state, a way of thinking, or a situation where we may feel really angry, lose control, and/or escalate. Becoming aware of these red flag signals helps us remain in control of ourselves and behaviors.

Physical Red Flags

What physical cues (cues in your body) will tell you that you are getting really angry and beginning to escalate?

- Muscle tension
- Heartbeat
- Disorientation

Self-Talk Red Flags

What kind of self-talk do you begin to have when your anger is rising and you are beginning to escalate?

- *He's trying to make a fool of me.*
- *He doesn't love me anymore.*
- *I think he wants to leave me.*
- *Are you seriously expecting me to do that for you?*
- *Somebody needs to teach him a lesson!*

Situational Red Flags

- Paying bills
- Hearing certain questions
- Dealing with kids
- After having a few drinks

What are the situations that are almost sure to start an argument between you and your partner?

When you know what these are, you can plan a whole lot better—either by avoiding some of them, or by being extra careful to monitor your own behavior.

SESSION 1 HOMEWORK #1

Handout

Identify three examples from the Female Abuse Wheel that you have engaged in with your partner. Be specific:

1.

2.

3.

SESSION 1 HOMEWORK #2

◆ **Handout**

Fill this out in preparation for the next session:

ANGER STYLES QUIZ

1.	I try never to get angry.	YES	NO
2.	I get really nervous when others are angry.	YES	NO
3.	I feel I'm doing something bad when I get angry.	YES	NO
4.	I often tell people I'll do what they want, but then I forget.	YES	NO
5.	I frequently say things like "Yeah, but . . . " and "I'll do it later."	YES	NO
6.	People tell me I must be angry but I'm not sure why.	YES	NO
7.	I get mad at myself a lot.	YES	NO
8.	I "stuff" my anger and then get headaches, stomachaches, etc.	YES	NO
9.	I frequently call myself ugly names like "dummy, selfish, etc."	YES	NO
10.	My anger comes on really fast.	YES	NO
11.	I act before I think when I get angry.	YES	NO
12.	My anger goes away very quickly.	YES	NO
13.	I get very angry when people criticize me.	YES	NO
14.	People say I am easily hurt and oversensitive.	YES	NO
15.	I get angry easily when I feel bad about myself.	YES	NO
16.	I get mad in order to get what I want.	YES	NO
17.	I try to scare others with my anger.	YES	NO
18.	I sometimes pretend to be mad when I'm not really angry.	YES	NO
19.	Sometimes I get angry just for the excitement or action.	YES	NO
20.	I like the strong feelings that come with my anger.	YES	NO
21.	Sometimes when I am bored I start arguments or pick fights.	YES	NO
22.	I seem to get angry all the time.	YES	NO
23.	My anger feels like a bad habit I have trouble breaking.	YES	NO
24.	I get mad without thinking—it feels automatic.	YES	NO
25.	I get jealous a lot, even when there is no reason.	YES	NO
26.	I don't trust people very much.	YES	NO
27.	Sometimes it feels like people are out to get me.	YES	NO

28.	I become very angry when I defend my beliefs and opinions.	YES	NO
29.	I often feel outraged about what others try to get away with.	YES	NO
30.	I always know I'm right in an argument.	YES	NO
31.	I hang onto my anger for a long time.	YES	NO
32.	I have a hard time forgiving people.	YES	NO
33.	I hate people for what they've done to me.	YES	NO

Adapted with permission from Potter-Efron, R., & Potter-Efron, P. (2006). Letting go of anger: The eleven most common anger styles and what to do about them. Oakland, CA: New Harbinger.

WHAT'S YOUR ANGER STYLE?

◆ Handout

Adapted with permission from Potter-Efron, R., & Potter-Efron, P. (2006). Letting go of anger: The eleven most common anger styles and what to do about them. Oakland, CA: New Harbinger.

I. **HIDDEN STYLES. These individuals are partly or mostly unaware/unaccepting of their anger.**
   A. *ANGER AVOIDANCE:* People who believe anger is bad, scary, or useless. They cannot use anger appropriately in their daily lives.
   Treatment Approaches: Assertiveness, separate concepts of selfishness from self-caring, permission to be angry.
   B. *SNEAKY ANGER:* Passive-aggressive individuals whose power centers on frustrating others through inaction.
   Treatment Approaches: Learn to say *yes* and *no*; focus upon positive goals; work with person's developmental history to seek sources of passivity.
   C. *ANGER TURNED INWARD:* These people frequently become angry at themselves, sometimes in self-destructive patterns.
   Treatment Approaches: Permission to externalize anger if appropriate; improved self-caring.

II. **EXPLOSIVE STYLES. These individuals periodically demonstrate their anger and aggression through dramatic outbursts.**
   A. *SUDDEN ANGER:* Anger comes out as rapid, usually short-lived, intense bursts.
   Treatment Approaches: Slow down the anger, time-outs, gain awareness of buildup stage.
   B. *SHAME-BASED ANGER:* Anger reflects perceived attacks upon a person's core self.
   Treatment Approaches: Address shame-rage connection, self-esteem imprvement, address shame-blame issues.
   C. *DELIBERATE ANGER:* Anger that is purposely displayed in order to intimidate.
   Treatment Approaches: Discuss gains and losses of this behavior, empathy training, teach alternative communication skills.
   D. *EXCITATORY ANGER:* Individuals seek the intensity of the anger rush.
   Treatment Approaches: Commitment to calmness and moderation, new lifestyle, connect to stimulant addiction pattern.

III. **CHRONIC STYLES. These people have developed long-term anger patterns that keep them angry, bitter, and resentful.**
   A. *HABITUAL ANGER:* Automatic thoughts and actions perpetuate nonfunctional anger.
   Treatment Approaches: Increased awareness of behavior, focus upon person's choices, practice new behavior.
   B. *PARANOIA:* Anger projected onto others and then defended against with defensive anger and aggression.

Treatment Approaches: Owning your anger, ending vigilance and proof-seeking behavior, developing trust.

C. *MORAL ANGER:* Anger is perceived as justified, righteous, for a cause greater than self-interest.
Treatment Approaches: Empathy to de-"devilize" others, emphasis on humanity and equality.

D. *RESENTMENT/HATE:* Others are treated as loathsome and unforgivable.
Treatment Approaches: Forgiveness as a gift to oneself, letting go of the past, resentment prevention.

THE FOUR-SQUARE TECHNIQUE

Handout

The Four-Square Technique is especially valuable when you are trying to make a decision about how to act. It might be something of major consequence, like whether to be violent with someone, or more of an everyday experience, like how to express your disappointment or unhappiness with one of your kids.

Every decision you make involves four outcomes to consider:

SHORT TERM/SELF	LONG TERM/SELF
SHORT TERM/PARTNER	LONG TERM/PARTNER

For example, if you are tempted to get drunk at a party (but your boyfriend often suffers when you do this), your Four-Square might look like this:

SHORT TERM/SELF	LONG TERM/SELF
GREAT!	GUILTY
SHORT TERM/ PARTNER	LONG TERM/PARTNER
HURTFUL	ANGRY/MISTRUSTING

Practically everything that you are tempted to do, like getting angry or aggressive, means that the Short Term/Self square is very appealing—otherwise you wouldn't be so tempted to do it. But, before you act, it is very important to consider the other three squares. *Will this be a good decision for other people? Will this be a good decision for me in the long run?*

If the vote on the Four-Square is 3 to 1 against, or even 2 to 2, it is usually a good idea *not* to go there.

HEALTHY ANGER/DESTRUCTIVE AGGRESSION

Handout

Everyone gets mad. Anger can be positive if it helps you stand up for yourself or makes things better.

Anger is healthy when . . .

. . . It doesn't turn into physical or verbal aggression.

. . . You take responsibility for your feelings. ("I'm angry," not "You make me mad.")

. . . It's about issues and not personalities. ("I need you to clean up after yourself," not "You're the most selfish person in the universe.")

. . . It lasts a short time and doesn't grow into resentment or grudges; and you can express your anger without saying or doing things that hurt you or others.

When you're angry, it's not okay to . . .

- Hit people
- Hit things
- Scream
- Push or shove
- Name-call
- Threaten
- Throw things
- Slam doors
- Blame
- Become reckless
- Take it out on others
- Draw others into the problem
- Ask others to choose sides
- Hurt yourself

When you're angry, it IS okay to . . .

- Splash water on your face
- Talk to yourself in the mirror
- Cry
- Walk away
- Write an angry letter and tear it up
- Take a time-out
- Send an I-message to tell the person that you are angry
- Ask the person to stop their behavior
- Talk it over with a friend
- Take a deep breath, and hold it in for as long as you can, then let it out as slowly as you can

LETTING GO OF ANGER

Handout

Anger is a part of life. Our wish for you, and for ourselves, is to be able to accept the blessing of anger, to listen to its message, and then let go of it.

DO'S AND DON'TS FOR TREATING OTHERS WITH RESPECT

Do . . .

- Begin each day with a promise to respect others.
- Sit down and talk quietly and listen carefully to what others say.
- Look for things to appreciate in others.
- Give praise out loud for the good you see in others.
- Tell others they are good, good enough, and lovable.
- Tell others they are worthwhile and important to you.
- Speak in a quiet voice even when you disagree.
- Pass up chances to insult, attack, or criticize.
- Let others have responsibility for their lives while you take responsibility for yours.

Don't . . .

- Look for things to criticize.
- Make fun or laugh at others.
- Make faces or roll your eyes.
- Tell others how to run their lives.
- Insult others.
- Ignore others.
- Put people down in front of others.
- Act superior.
- Sneer.
- Tell others they're weird or crazy.
- Say others are bad, not good enough, or unlovable.
- Say others don't belong or you wish they were dead.
- Call others names like *fat, ugly, stupid*, or *worthless*.

SESSION 2 HOMEWORK

Handout

Review the handout on Healthy Anger/Destructive Aggression. Think of three items on the list of "When You're Angry, It's Okay To . . ." that have worked for you in the past. Then write down three more of your own that aren't on the list:

1.

2.

3.

PUT-DOWNS FROM PARENTS

◆ Handout

Adapted with permission from Dutton, D. G. (1998). The abusive personality: Violence and control in intimate relationships. New York: Guilford Press.

Please write in the number listed below (1–4) that best describes how often the experience happened to you with your mother (or stepmother, female guardian, etc.) and father (or stepfather, male guardian, etc.) when you were growing up. If you had more than one mother or father figure, please answer for the persons whom you feel played the most important role in your upbringing.

You might choose to share your responses with the group, but that decision will be *completely* up to you. The more honest you can be as you describe yourself and your history, the more you will be able to benefit from this program.

1	2	3	4
Never Occurred	Occasionally Occurred	Sometimes Occurred	Frequently Occurred

Father   Mother

1. I think that my parent wished I had been a really different kind of child.   _____ _____
2. As a child, I was physically punished or scolded in the presence of others.   _____ _____
3. I was treated as the scapegoat of the family.   _____ _____
4. I felt my parent thought it was my fault when he/she was unhappy.   _____ _____
5. I think my parent was mean and held grudges towards me.   _____ _____
6. I was punished by my parents without having done anything.   _____ _____
7. My parent criticized me and/or told me how useless I was in front of others.   _____ _____
8. My parent beat me for no reason.   _____ _____
9. My parent would be angry with me without letting me know why.   _____ _____

FORGIVING THE SELF

Handout

Guilt is the feeling that lets us know when we have made a mistake or violated our own values—feeling guilty can be a very healthy way of motivating us to change.

Guilt = I made a mistake

Shame is the belief—and the horrible feelings that come with it—that we are fundamentally defective.

Shame = I AM a mistake

SHAME	GUILT
I am a failure.	*I failed to do something.*
Everything I do is wrong.	*I make mistakes sometimes.*
This can never be repaired.	*Forgiveness and amends often lead to healing and repair.*
I have to keep this horrible thing secret.	*If I can find someone to talk to about this, I can learn, recover, and grow.*

You can forgive yourself for your mistakes (and release yourself from shame) when you can . . .

1. Stop the behavior.
2. Acknowledge what you did and that you do not want to do it again.
3. Acknowledge that you hurt yourself and/or others.
4. Make amends to others, when possible and appropriate.
5. Explore alternative behaviors that honor your feelings and are respectful to self and others.
6. Move forward in a manner that honors the wisdom you now have and the life you wish for yourself.

SESSION 3 HOMEWORK

◆ Handout

Fill out the Put-Downs from Parents chart again, this time from the perspective of one of your own children. If you do not have children, pick a child you know well and try to fill it out from his or her perspective.

1	2	3	4
Never Occurred	Occasionally Occurred	Sometimes Occurred	Frequently Occurred

                                                                                                                                                   Father Mother

1. I think that my parent wished I had been a really different kind of child.   _____ _____

2. As a child, I was physically punished or scolded in the presence of others.   _____ _____

3. I was treated as the scapegoat of the family.   _____ _____

4. I felt my parent thought it was my fault when he/she was unhappy.   _____ _____

5. I think my parent was mean and held grudges towards me.   _____ _____

6. I was punished by my parents without having done anything.   _____ _____

7. My parent criticized me and/or told me how useless I was in front of others.   _____ _____

8. My parent beat me for no reason.   _____ _____

9. My parent would be angry with me without letting me know why.   _____ _____

ADVERSE CHILDHOOD EXPERIENCES (ACE) INFO

◆ Handout

- Adverse Childhood Experiences (ACEs) are very common.
- ACEs are strong predictors of later health risks.
- This combination makes ACEs one of the leading predictors of adult health and social well-being.

1. The original ACE study was conducted on 17,337 participants from the Kaiser health care system between 1995 and 1997.

2. About 67% of individuals reported at least one ACE. If someone had one ACE point, they usually had more: 87% who reported one ACE reported at least one additional ACE.

3. The number of childhood ACEs was strongly associated with adult problems with . . .
   - smoking
   - alcohol and drug abuse
   - sexual promiscuity
   - severe obesity
   - depression
   - heart disease
   - cancer
   - chronic lung disease
   - shortened life span
   - domestic violence

4. Compared to an ACE score of zero, having four ACE points is associated with a sevenfold increase in alcoholism, a doubling of risk of being diagnosed with cancer, and a fourfold increase in emphysema.

5. ACE scores above six are associated with a 30-fold increase in attempted suicide.

ACE Score and the Risk of *Perpetrating* Domestic Violence

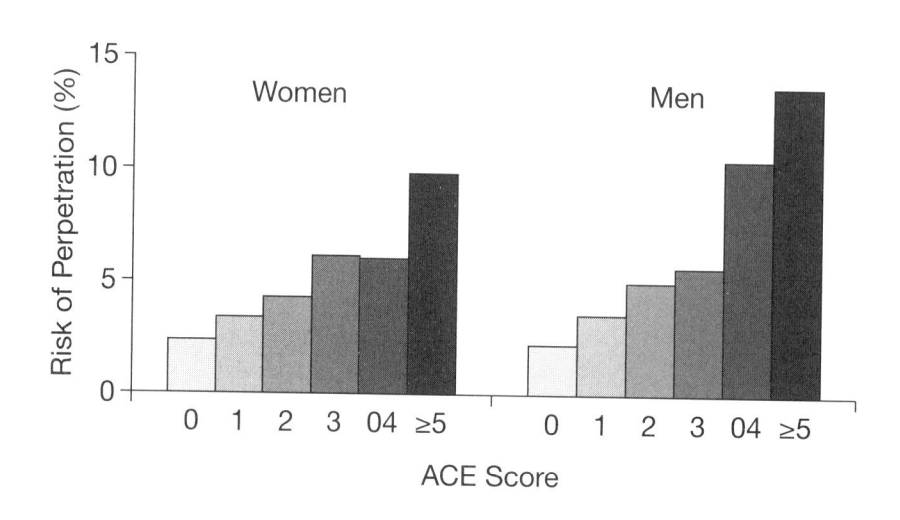

Source: Based on information from Whitfield, C. L., Anda, R. F., Dube, S. R., & Felitti, V. J. (2003). Violent childhood experiences and the risk of intimate partner violence in adults: Assessment in a large health maintenance organization. Journal of Interpersonal Violence, 18(2), 166–185.

WHAT'S MY ACE SCORE?

◆ **Handout**

Prior to your 18th birthday:

1. Did a parent or other adult in the household often or very often . . .
Swear at you, insult you, put you down, or humiliate you?
or
Act in a way that made you afraid that you might be physically hurt?
          Yes No   If yes, enter 1 _____

2. Did a parent or other adult in the household often or very often . . .
Push, grab, slap, or throw something at you?
or
Ever hit you so hard that you had marks or were injured?
          Yes No   If yes, enter 1 _____

3. Did an adult or person at least five years older than you ever . . .
Touch or fondle you or have you touch their body in a sexual way?
or
Attempt or actually have oral, anal, or vaginal intercourse with you?
          Yes No   If yes, enter 1 _____

4. Did you often or very often feel that . . .
No one in your family loved you or thought you
were important or special?
or
Your family didn't look out for each other, feel
close to each other, or support each other?
          Yes No   If yes, enter 1 _____

5. Did you often or very often feel that . . .
You didn't have enough to eat, had to wear dirty clothes,
and had no one to protect you?
or
Your parents were too drunk or high to take care of you or
take you to the doctor if you needed it?
          Yes No   If yes, enter 1 _____

6. Were your parents ever separated or divorced?
          Yes No   If yes, enter 1 _____

7. Was your mother or stepmother (or father or stepfather):
Often or very often pushed, grabbed, slapped, or had something thrown at her (or him)?
      or
Sometimes, often, or very often kicked, bitten, hit with a fist, or hit with something hard?
      or
Ever hit repeatedly over at least a few minutes or threatened with a gun or knife?

                                      Yes   No   If yes, enter 1 _____

8. Did you live with anyone who was a problem drinker or alcoholic, or who used street drugs?

                                      Yes   No   If yes, enter 1 _____

9. Was a household member depressed or mentally ill, or did a household member attempt suicide?

                                      Yes   No   If yes, enter 1 _____

10. Did a household member go to prison?

                                      Yes   No   If yes, enter 1 _____

                        Now add up your Yes answers: _____ This is your ACE score.

Originally published in Felitti, V. J., Anda, R. F., Nordenberg, D., Williamson, D. F., Spitz, A. M., Edwards, V., Koss, M. P., & Marks, J. S. (1998). Relationship of Childhood Abuse and Household Dysfunction to Many of the Leading Causes of Death in Adults: The Adverse Childhood Experiences (ACE) Study. American Journal of Preventive Medicine, 14, 245–258.

ACE RESILIENCE QUESTIONNAIRE

◆ Handout

Many childhood experiences have been found to help cushion the impact of ACE scores. These usually help protect most people with four or more ACEs from developing negative outcomes.

1. I believe that my mother loved me when I was little.
   Definitely true   Prob true   Not sure   Prob not true   Def not true

2. I believe that my father loved me when I was little.
   Definitely true   Prob true   Not sure   Prob not true   Def not true

3. When I was little, other people helped my mother and father take care of me, and they seemed to love me.
   Definitely true   Prob true   Not sure   Prob not true   Def not true

4. I've heard that when I was an infant someone in my family enjoyed playing with me, and I enjoyed it too.
   Definitely true   Prob true   Not sure   Prob not true   Def not true

5. When I was a child, there were relatives in my family who made me feel better if I was sad or worried.
   Definitely true   Prob true   Not sure   Prob not true   Def not true

6. When I was a child, neighbors or my friends' parents seemed to like me.
   Definitely true   Prob true   Not sure   Prob not true   Def not true

7. When I was a child, teachers, coaches, youth leaders, or ministers were there to help me.
   Definitely true   Prob true   Not sure   Prob not true   Def not true

8. Someone in my family cared about how I was doing in school.
   Definitely true   Prob true   Not sure   Prob not true   Def not true

9. My family, neighbors, and friends talked often about making our lives better.
   Definitely true   Prob true   Not sure   Prob not true   Def not true

10. We had rules in our house and were expected to keep them.
    Definitely true   Prob true   Not sure   Prob not true   Def not true

11. When I felt really bad, I could almost always find someone I trusted to talk to.
    Definitely true   Prob true   Not sure   Prob not true   Def not true

12. As a youth, people noticed that I was capable and could get things done.

    Definitely true   Prob true   Not sure   Prob not true   Def not true

13. I was independent and a go-getter.

    Definitely true   Prob true   Not sure   Prob not true   Def not true

14. I believed that life is what you make it.

    Definitely true   Prob true   Not sure   Prob not true   Def not true

How many of these 14 protective factors did I have as a child and youth? (How many of the 14 were circled "Definitely True" or "Prob True"?) _____

SESSION 4 HOMEWORK

◆ Handout

Fill out the What's My ACE Score? questionnaire again, this time from the perspective of one of your own children. If you do not have children, pick a child you know well and try to fill it out from his or her perspective.

Then do the same with the ACE Resilience Questionnaire, again from the child's perspective.

What's My ACE Score?

Prior to your 18th birthday:

1. Did a parent or other adult in the household often or very often . . .
   Swear at you, insult you, put you down, or humiliate you?
       or
   Act in a way that made you afraid that you might be physically hurt?
                                        Yes   No   If yes, enter 1 _____

2. Did a parent or other adult in the household often or very often . . .
   Push, grab, slap, or throw something at you?
       or
   Ever hit you so hard that you had marks or were injured?
                                        Yes   No   If yes, enter 1 _____

3. Did an adult or person at least 5 years older than you ever . . .
   Touch or fondle you or have you touch their body in a sexual way?
       or
   Attempt or actually have oral, anal, or vaginal intercourse with you?
                                        Yes   No   If yes, enter 1 _____

4. Did you often or very often feel that . . .
   No one in your family loved you or thought you
   were important or special?
       or
   Your family didn't look out for each other, feel
   close to each other, or support each other?
                                        Yes   No   If yes, enter 1 _____

5. Did you often or very often feel that . . .
   You didn't have enough to eat, had to wear dirty clothes,
   and had no one to protect you?
       or
   Your parents were too drunk or high to take care of you or
   take you to the doctor if you needed it?
                                        Yes   No   If yes, enter 1 _____

6. Was a biological parent ever lost to you through divorce, abandonment, or other reason?

                                                                                  Yes   No   If yes, enter 1 _____

7. Was your mother or stepmother (or father or stepfather):
Often or very often pushed, grabbed, slapped, or had something thrown at her (or him)?
        or
Sometimes, often, or very often kicked, bitten, hit with a fist, or hit with something hard?
        or
Ever hit repeatedly over at least a few minutes or threatened with a gun or knife?

                                                                                   Yes   No   If yes, enter 1 _____

8. Did you live with anyone who was a problem drinker or alcoholic, or who used street drugs?

                                                                                  Yes   No   If yes, enter 1 _____

9. Was a household member depressed or mentally ill, or did a household member attempt suicide?

                                                                                  Yes   No   If yes, enter 1 _____

10. Did a household member go to prison?

                                                                                  Yes   No   If yes, enter 1 _____

Now add up your Yes answers: _____ This is your ACE score.

ACE RESILIENCE QUESTIONNAIRE

Handout

Many childhood experiences have been found to help cushion the impact of ACE scores. These usually help protect most people with four or more ACEs from developing negative outcomes.

1. I believe that my mother loved me when I was little.
    Definitely true   Prob true   Not sure   Prob not true   Def not true

2. I believe that my father loved me when I was little.
    Definitely true   Prob true   Not sure   Prob not true   Def not true

3. When I was little, other people helped my mother and father take care of me, and they seemed to love me.
    Definitely true   Prob true   Not sure   Prob not true   Def not true

4. I've heard that when I was an infant someone in my family enjoyed playing with me, and I enjoyed it, too.
    Definitely true   Prob true   Not sure   Prob not true   Def not true

5. When I was a child, there were relatives in my family who made me feel better if I was sad or worried.
    Definitely true   Prob true   Not sure   Prob not true   Def not true

6. When I was a child, neighbors or my friends' parents seemed to like me.
    Definitely true   Prob true   Not sure   Prob not true   Def not true

7. When I was a child, teachers, coaches, youth leaders, or ministers were there to help me.
    Definitely true   Prob true   Not sure   Prob not true   Def not true

8. Someone in my family cared about how I was doing in school.
    Definitely true   Prob true   Not sure   Prob not true   Def not true

9. My family, neighbors, and friends talked often about making our lives better.
    Definitely true   Prob true   Not sure   Prob not true   Def not true

10. We had rules in our house and were expected to keep them.
    Definitely true   Prob true   Not sure   Prob not true   Def not true

11. When I felt really bad, I could almost always find someone I trusted to talk to.
    Definitely true   Prob true   Not sure   Prob not true   Def not true

12. As a youth, people noticed that I was capable and could get things done.
   Definitely true   Prob true   Not sure   Prob not true   Def not true

13. I was independent and a go-getter.
   Definitely true   Prob true   Not sure   Prob not true   Def not true

14. I believed that life is what you make it.
   Definitely true   Prob true   Not sure   Prob not true   Def not true

How many of these 14 protective factors did I have as a child and youth? (How many of the 14 were circled "Definitely True" or "Prob True"?) _____

THINKING THE WORST

Handout

WHAT HAPPENED? WHAT ARE THE EFFECTS?	THE STORY YOU TELL YOURSELF
Trauma happened	▪ *Nowhere is safe.* ▪ *The next disaster will strike soon.*
Trauma happened *to me*	▪ *I attract disaster.* ▪ *People can see that I am a victim.* ▪ *I deserve bad things to happen to me.* ▪ *My personality has gotten worse.*
Irritability/anger/outbursts	▪ *My marriage won't make it.* ▪ *I can't trust myself with my own kids.*
Emotional numbing	▪ *I'm dead inside.* ▪ *I'll never relate okay to people again.*
Difficulty concentrating	▪ *I'll never get over this.* ▪ *My brain has been permanently damaged.* ▪ *I'll lose my job.*
Positive reactions from others	▪ *They think I'm too weak to cope—that's why they're trying to help me.* ▪ *I don't want anyone's pity.*
Negative reactions from others	▪ *They are judging me for what happened to me.* ▪ *Nobody's there for me and never will be.* ▪ *I can't rely on other people.*
Physical consequences	▪ *My body is ruined.* ▪ *I'll never lead a normal life again.*

THE STORIES OF TRAUMA

◆ Handout

If you can identify a traumatic event, take a few moments to make some notes about why you think this traumatic event occurred. For example: *I was sexually assaulted because of the way I dressed,* or *I did a lot of bad things as a kid, which is why I keep losing people who are close to me.*

It might be more comfortable to choose a more moderate event, like the breakup of a relationship (which practically everyone has experienced).

Also—remember that not all traumas are created equal. You may never have experienced extreme, dramatic trauma (like soldiers in combat zones or a violent childhood), but you have still been affected by the events in your own life.

You are not being asked to write specifics about the traumatic event. Write what you have been thinking you may have done that caused this event.

When you are done, we will discuss examples in the group. We want to make sure that no one in this group holds on to distorted reasons for why bad things have happened in their lives.

TRAUMATIC EVENT:

THIS HAPPENED BECAUSE . . .

SESSION 5 HOMEWORK

◆ Handout

Think of someone you know who has experienced a traumatic event, like a rape or growing up in a violent family. Write 100 words of what you would say to that person about why this happened. See if you can focus on the message that this was *not* his or her fault.

WHAT YOU WOULD SAY (100 WORDS):

GIRLFRIENDS AND SOCIAL SUPPORT

◆ Handout

Adapted with permission from Koonin, M., Cabarcas, A., & Geffner, R. (2002). Women Ending Abusive/Violent Episodes Respectfully (WEAVER) Manual. San Diego CA: Family Violence and Sexual Assault Institute.

Women who have been most supportive in your life are:

What actions did these women do that made you feel supported?

What qualities have you admired in other women?

When do you or your friends justify violence? (For example: when your partner is caught cheating, when a friend is intimate with your partner, when someone threatens your child)

Have you disclosed to your friends that you are in a domestic violence group or have been aggressive to your partner?

Have your friends encouraged your violence or helped you validate it?

Women tend to be very supportive of one another. Do you have friends that will honestly challenge you when you are in the wrong or acting out of hand?

THE HOUSE OF SELF-WORTH AND EMPOWERMENT

Self-Worth   *Empowerment*

Parenting	Job	Relaxation
Partner Relationship		Personal Integrity
Spirituality	Personal Skills	Social Life

SESSION 6 HOMEWORK

◆ Handout

MAKING CHANGES

Adapted with permission from Koonin, M., Cabarcas, A., & Geffner, R. (2002). Women Ending Abusive/Violent Episodes Respectfully (WEAVER) Manual. San Diego CA: Family Violence and Sexual Assault Institute.

Check any boxes to the right that are goals of yours (and fill in the specifics in that box if you see a . . .). Then make notes about when you expect to see progress on this, what seems to be in the way, and what resources you need to move forward.

GOAL	BY WHEN?	OBSTACLES?	RESOURCES NEEDED?
Finish school			
Do work as . . .			
Be recognized as . . .			
Be in a stable relationship			
Have children			

People I want to know . . .			
Places I want to see . . .			
Skills I want to learn . . .			
Add or lose ___ pounds			
Other goals . . .			

BAD RAP

◆ Handout

Adapted with permission from Wexler, D. B. (1991). The adolescent self: Strategies for self-management, self-soothing, and self-esteem in adolescence. New York: Norton.

1. **BLACK AND WHITE:** Seeing things as all or nothing: *never/always/everyone.*

    A good woman is always there to help.
    You're either on my side or you're not.
    You can't trust men.

2. **MINIMIZING:** Downplaying your achievements.

    Even though I finally made supervisor, it's no big deal.
    I did well, but so did a lot of other people.
    My counselor just gives me good feedback because she's paid to say it.

3. **MIND READING:** Assuming that others think something without checking it out.

    I know my boss hates me—he gave me a dirty look.
    He's avoiding me—he must be pretty mad.
    My partner didn't call me today—she must not care about me.

4. **AWFULIZING:** Predicting that things will turn out awful for you.

    My boss will never trust me again.
    I know I'm not going to make it through this place.
    Wow, she is so good at that—I'll never be able to do it that well!

5. **ERROR IN BLAMING:** Unfairly blaming yourself—or others.

    It's all my fault, or *It's all your fault.*
    It's my fault my son is shy.
    You always mess everything up for me.

6. **DOWN-PUTTING:** Making too much of your mistakes (opposite of **MINIMIZING**).

    I failed this test; I must be dumb.
    I'm in counseling; there must be something really wrong with me.
    She doesn't like me, so there must be something really wrong with me.

7. **EMOTIONAL REASONING:** Concluding that if you *feel* a certain way about yourself, then it must be true.

    Since I feel bad about myself, I must be a bad person.
    I feel rejected, so everybody must be rejecting me.
    Since I feel guilty, I must have done something wrong.

BAD RAP QUIZ

◆ **Handout**

Adapted with permission from Wexler, D. B. (1991). The adolescent self: Strategies for self-management, self-soothing, and self-esteem in adolescence. New York: Norton.

1. The counselor told me I'm doing better, but I know he tells that to everybody.
2. Ever since that really handsome guy Paul hurt me, I know that good-looking men can't be trusted.
3. If I'm angry, there must be something to be angry about.
4. Nothing's ever going to work out for me.
5. It's your fault we never do anything fun.
6. My parents got divorced; it must have been something about me.
7. I sometimes don't get things right, so I must be lazy or stupid.
8. I feel lonely, so I guess nobody likes me.
9. That supervisor shows me no respect; nobody in this organization cares a damn about me.

STORIES WE TELL OURSELVES

◆ Handout

THE OLD STORY	THE NEW STORY
If he forgets my birthday, it means he doesn't love me.	I feel hurt when he forgets my birthday, but there are other ways he shows me he loves me.
I can't believe my son violated curfew. He's always pushing the limits with me—and I have to teach him a lesson!	I'm glad he's safe—in the morning I can talk calmly with him and figure out what happened and what to do.
He always has to win every argument. He just wants to show how he's smarter than I am!	He does have strong opinions, but so do I. I don't always have to change my mind—or his.
She's trying to start a fight with me to make me act crazy! She wants to get me arrested!	I don't have to get into a fight with her, and I don't have to choose violence.
My daughter always expects me to help her with her homework—she's such a baby!	Learning to read is hard. I'm glad she turns to me for help, and I'm glad I can help her.
If he doesn't listen to me, I'll throw the remote at him—it's the only way to get his attention!	Relationships are not always easy, and violence isn't going to bring us closer. I don't want to make a bad situation even worse.

SESSION 7 HOMEWORK

Handout

Go back to the Stories We Tell Ourselves chart. Fill out three more examples (from your personal experience) that could go on this list.

1.

2.

3.

JEALOUSY: TAMING THE GREEN-EYED MONSTER

◆ Handout

Jealousy is one of those emotions that can tie our stomach in knots in a hurry. A little bit of jealousy is natural, especially when we fear losing someone close to us. Jealousy becomes a problem when . . .

- we spend too much energy worrying about losing a loved one
- we let jealousy build, and we try to control someone else through aggression
- we stifle a relationship by placing extreme restrictions on our partner

Tania got herself really worked up whenever she went to a party with her husband, Peter. Tania was afraid that he would find another woman more attractive and exciting than she was. She usually picked some sort of fight with him after the party, without ever telling him what she was really upset about.

One day after one of these fights, Tania was thinking about how upset she made herself with jealousy. She tried to look at the situation in a more objective way—the way an outside observer would. After a while she was able to say to herself, *My husband is very attractive, and it is only natural that women will sometimes find him attractive too. That doesn't mean I'm going to lose him. He hasn't given me any reason to doubt him. My fears and anger come from doubting my self-worth. If other women like him, it only confirms what I already know—and that's positive.*

Alicia's jealousy was even stronger than Tania's. She would question her boyfriend at length when he came home, asking where he had been, who he had been with, and the details of his activities. She checked out his text messages and his phone bills. She would get urges to follow him everywhere or demand that he stay home. It seemed that the more she questioned him, the more she disbelieved him.

It was after hearing her friend talk about wanting to have an affair that Alicia realized what was happening. The times when she was most suspicious of her boyfriend were the times when *she* was actually thinking about other men.

Now when she noticed jealousy, she asked herself, *Am I just thinking that he's cheating on me because I'm feeling guilty?*

Amy found that the best way for her to tame the monster was to let her girlfriend know when she felt jealous. She felt very relieved being able to talk about it. Sometimes they could laugh about it together. Instead of responding with ridicule, she seemed to respect her more. Both of them went on to say what behavior from each other they could and could not tolerate—affairs, flirting, having friends, and so on. They were able to work out some contracts that specified the limits of the relationship.

What **Tania, Alicia,** and **Amy** learned about taming jealousy was the following:

1. Some jealousy is normal, and it's best to talk about it rather than hide it.

2. People can choose to see their partner's attractiveness and behavior in the most negative possible way—or they can turn it around and see it in a way that is not such a threat.

3. It will help people to ask, *Is my jealousy coming from my guilt about my own fantasies or behavior?*

4. Women have the right to request and contract for some specific limits on their partner's behavior (not thoughts), and men have the same right.*

---

* Thanks to Daniel G. Saunders, PhD, for contributing many of these ideas.

STORIES OF JEALOUSY: I KNEW I WAS RIGHT

◆ Handout

Maria had been cheated on in the past. She was "sure" that men couldn't be trusted. It seemed like all her friends had been through the same thing.

She knew it was just a matter of time until her boyfriend Antonio would betray her, and she knew that she needed to watch him carefully. When she did his laundry, she'd check his pockets for receipts and phone numbers. When she drove his car, she'd check the mileage to see how far he had gone. She figured out the password for his phone and email and checked it regularly without him knowing about it.

If he put on nice clothes and cologne, she would grill him about where he was going, because she knew that he must be getting dressed up to meet another woman.

Eventually, Antonio got really tired of Maria checking on him all the time—and he actually began seeing someone else who wasn't so jealous and insecure. Maria's story about men was confirmed: this proved that men couldn't be trusted, and that she was right—again—about this one. She began following him around to see who this other woman was and whether she was prettier than Maria.

Sometimes we actually want something to go wrong in our relationships—just so we can say that we knew we were right all along.

SESSION 8 HOMEWORK

Handout

Record three experiences of jealousy over the next week. These can include anything from high levels (like seeing your husband or partner flirting with someone else) to low (like observing your supervisor give approval to someone else). If you do not notice any this week, recall experiences from previous weeks.

1.

2.

3.

SWITCH!

Handout

1. ***What went wrong?***
   a. Who was involved? When was it? Where was it? Describe exactly what was happening. Be specific and objective.
   b. Replay this like a movie. What exactly did you do and say?
   c. Other group members should help by asking questions so the movie is very clear.

2. ***What was my OLD SELF-TALK?***
   a. What was your self-talk before, during, and after the situation?
   b. Freeze the frame of this movie so you can stop at different points and identify the self-talk.
   c. With the group's help, analyze the self-defeating or unproductive self-talk.

3. ***What NEW SELF-TALK could I have used?***
   a. What would you like to have said to yourself instead in this situation?
   b. Brainstorm with the group for alternative self-talk.

4. ***The Switch!***
   a. Put yourself back in the problem situation.
   b. Practice the OLD SELF-TALK out loud (see the notes on the board).
   c. When the group yells out "Switch!" try using your NEW SELF-TALK instead (see the notes on the board).

5. ***What do you think? What does the group think?***
   a. Do you think this would have led to a different outcome?
   b. Do you really think you could use this new self-talk in the future? What might get in your way?

SESSION 9 HOMEWORK

◆ Handout

Do your own Switch! exercise. Pick out another time when you wish you had not reacted the way you did in your relationship.

SITUATION AND YOUR REACTION

OLD SELF-TALK

NEW SELF-TALK

PREDICTED NEW REACTION

ASSERTIVENESS

◆ **Handout**

ASSERTIVENESS: TAKING CARE OF YOUR OWN NEEDS, THOUGHTS, AND FEELINGS—IN A WAY THAT IS LEAST LIKELY TO MAKE THE OTHER PERSON FEEL ATTACKED OR ACT DEFENSIVE

1. **Assertive.** This behavior involves knowing what you feel and want. It also involves expressing your feelings and needs directly and honestly without violating the rights of others. At all times you are accepting responsibility for your feelings and actions.
   - "It bothered me when you were late coming back from shopping, because I had to rush off to work."

2. **Aggressive.** You attack your partner, act controlling, provoke a confrontation, and maybe even get violent. The consequences could be destructive to others as well as yourself.
   - "What the hell's wrong with you? All you ever think about is yourself!"

3. **Passive.** You withdraw, become anxious, and avoid confrontation. You let others think for you, make decisions for you, and tell you what to do. You feel resentful but don't express it or deal with it. You feel like it's useless: either you don't deserve any better, or nobody will ever listen to you anyway. Usually you will become depressed, and you may believe that your partner is purposely trying to take advantage of you—but you do nothing about the situation.
   - "That's OK, whatever you want."

4. **Passive-Aggressive.** In this behavior you are not direct in relating to people, do not accept what is happening—but will retaliate in an indirect manner. This type of behavior can cause confusion. The other person feels stung but can't be exactly sure how or why. And you can act like you have done nothing at all—and imply that your partner is just too sensitive.
   - You act cold to your partner, then pretend like nothing's wrong when he or she asks you about it.
   - A woman feels unappreciated by her husband and "forgets" to give him a message.
   - A woman makes some "joking" comment about her partner's weight.

5. SPECIAL CATEGORY: **Passive-Assertive.** There are plenty of situations when someone assertively chooses to be passive. And this is often a good choice. When one person is in a bad mood and complaining about things that are not really fair, sometimes—in the most successful of relationships—the other partner just chooses to let it go. The same is true when an employee chooses to keep her mouth shut even when she doesn't like an office policy (thanks to Genevieve Olucha, PhD, for this concept).

WHAT IS ASSERTIVE BEHAVIOR?

◆ Handout

1. Asking for what you want but not being demanding.
2. Expressing feelings.
3. Genuinely expressing feedback or compliments to others and accepting them.
4. Disagreeing without being aggressive.
5. Asking questions and getting information from others.
6. Using I-messages and "I feel" statements without being judgmental or blaming.
7. Making eye contact during a conversation (unless this is inappropriate in the person's culture).

EXAMPLES:

1. *Can you give me some feedback about how I handled the kids' homework tonight?*
2. *I feel embarrassed when you tease me about my weight in front of my friends.*
3. *Mom, I know you want us to call more often, but I don't think you realize how busy we both are.*
4. *Corey, I just saw your report card, and I'm concerned. Let's sit down and talk about this together.*
5. *Maria, I'd like to talk about this later after we've both cooled off.*
6. Look your partner in the eye and say, *I really care about you. Let's work this out.*

BOUNDARY VIOLATIONS

Handout

Adapted with permission from Turner (Fischer, K. L. & McGrane, M. F. [1997]. Journey beyond abuse: A step-by-step guide to facilitating women's domestic abuse groups. St Paul: Amherst H. Wilder Foundation.).

TIME:
- Expecting partner to cease current activity in order to immediately meet the other partner's demands
- Setting a curfew for a partner
- Starting a fight as partner is leaving for work or another appointment

SPACE:
- Not treating purses, wallets, files, drawers, and so on as private space
- Making accusations about what your partner has been doing while away
- Getting too close physically when in conflict

PROPERTY:
- Taking or using things without asking
- Destruction of personal property, meant to be personally hurtful
- Taking car keys to prevent partner from leaving

PRIVACY:
- Reading/checking partner's mail, voicemail, or journal
- Listening in on phone conversations
- Demanding that partner account for all her/his time

SEXUAL:
- Lack of privacy in bathroom
- Making negative comments regarding partner's size and shape
- Not accepting when a partner says no to sex

FEELINGS:
- Telling partner what he/she should feel
- Calling partner wrong, ridiculous, bad, overly sensitive, and so on, because of how they feel
- Taunting, mimicking, or belittling partner for feelings

Recognizing boundary violations against yourself (and your own boundary violations of others) is the first step toward establishing more healthful boundaries.

SESSION 10 HOMEWORK

◆ Handout

WHERE IS YOUR LINE IN THE SAND?

We all put up with lots of imperfections and annoying behaviors in our partners. The capacity to do this is usually a sign of personal strength, maturity, and love. But some unacceptable behaviors are so profoundly unacceptable that they should never be tolerated, or at least never tolerated more than once. When you draw a line in the sand, you are making a contract with yourself that you will absolutely leave this relationship under certain conditions. When you put it in writing, and you sign it, you are more likely to have the perspective and courage to follow through if the situation actually happens.

I will have no choice but to leave my partner if he or she ever (cheats on me, hits me, abuses the children, lies to me about gambling, makes another suicide attempt, visits child porn sites, etc.):

1. _____
2. _____
3. _____

I will have no choice but to leave my partner if he or she ever no longer (talks to me for weeks on end, tries to find a job, allows me to talk on the phone with my friends or family, etc.):

1. _____
2. _____
3. _____

_____   _____
Your signature   Date

RESPECTFUL FEEDBACK

◆ Handout

Adapted with permission from Koonin, M., Cabarcas, A., & Geffner, R. (2002). Women Ending Abusive/Violent Episodes Respectfully (WEAVER) Manual. San Diego CA: Family Violence and Sexual Assault Institute.

The purpose of respectful feedback is to offer your partner some valuable information—not to make them feel attacked or beat up.

1. Feedback focuses on describing rather than judging behavior.
2. Feedback is specific rather than general.
3. Feedback takes into account the needs of both the receiver and giver of the feedback.
4. Feedback is directed toward behavior that the receiver can do something about.
5. Feedback is well timed.
6. Feedback is checked to ensure clear communication.
7. Both the giver and the receiver need to check with others, if possible, the accuracy of the feedback. Is this one person's impression or an impression shared by others?
8. Feedback contains only the amount of information that the receiver can tolerate.

ASKING FOR CHANGE

Handout

One method to use when you want to communicate your feelings, meanings, and intentions is I-messages. I-messages are specific, nonjudgmental, and focus on you. In contrast, you-messages are hostile, blaming, and focused on the other person. Reframing you-messages into I-messages can help you communicate—because the other person will not feel attacked.

Construct I-messages by using these phrases:

1. **When you** (just describe, don't blame).
2. **I feel** (state the feeling) **because** (explain in more detail).
   Note: Using the word *because* with an explanation can help by giving the other person more information to understand you.
3. **I wish** (specify a new behavior that you would like the other person to use instead).
4. **And if you can do that, I will** (explain how the other person will benefit).

The different parts of the I-message do not have to be delivered in exact order. The important thing is to keep the focus on yourself and to stay away from blame.

- *When you take long phone calls during dinner,*
- *I get angry because I begin to think you don't want to talk to me.*
- *I wish you would tell whoever's calling that you'll call back because we're in the middle of dinner.*
- *And if you can do that, I'll make sure not to hassle you about being on the phone later.*

- *When you don't come home or call,*
- *I get worried that something has happened to you.*
- *I would really like you to call me if you're going to be late.*
- *And if you can do that, I promise not to have an attitude when you get home.*

- *When you yell at me right in the middle of a busy time at work,*
- *I get so rattled that I end up making more mistakes.*
- *I wish that you would lighten up when you know that I'm busy.*
- *And if you can do that, I will be a lot easier to work with.*

CLASSIC MISTAKES:

1. Being too vague: *When you are selfish . . .*
2. Putting down character (*You are so controlling!*) instead of a specific behavior (*Last night it bothered me that you gave me so many instructions about the kids*).
3. Saying, *I feel that you . . .* instead of *I feel* (emotion).
4. Not offering a specific and realistic new behavior (*I want you to become a more outgoing person*).

HOW WE TALK OURSELVES OUT OF IT

◆ **Handout**

1. *I can't stand it if my partner gets upset with me.*
   NEW STORY:

2. *If I ask for help, I must be too needy.*
   NEW STORY:

3. *I don't deserve to get what I want or need.*
   NEW STORY:

4. *If I have to ask, it means he (or she) doesn't love me.*
   NEW STORY:

5. *I must really be a loser if I can't fix this myself.*
   NEW STORY:

6. *Making this request is a really pushy (bad, self-centered, selfish) thing to do.*
   NEW STORY:

7. *It doesn't make any difference. I don't care anyway.*
   NEW STORY:

8. *Obviously the problem is just in my head. If I would just think differently, I wouldn't have to bother someone else.*
   NEW STORY:

9. *Saying no is always a selfish thing.*
   NEW STORY:

SESSION 11 HOMEWORK

Handout

How often do you take full responsibility for what you do and say?
 Record two situations when you heard yourself say any of these types of statements (out loud or just in your own head):

- *You made me . . .*
- *It's your fault that I . . .*
- *If you (or he or she) weren't so XXXX, I wouldn't have to . . .*
- *I only did XXXX because I was drunk.*
- *He made me so mad that I had to . . .*

SITUATION #1:

What You Told Yourself That Gave Up Your Responsibility:

What You Could Have Said To Yourself Instead:

SITUATION #2:

What You Told Yourself That Gave Up Your Responsibility:

What You Could Have Said To Yourself Instead:

ACTIVE LISTENING

◆ Handout

Active listening is a communication technique that encourages the other person to continue speaking. It also enables you to be certain you understand what the other person is saying. It's a way of checking it out. It's called active listening because you not only listen but also actively let the other person know that you have really heard him or her.

A. Active listening involves PARAPHRASING.

Paraphrasing is stating in your own words what you think the other person has said.

- *You sound really* (feeling) *about* (situation).
- *You must really feel . . .* (state a feeling).
- *What I hear you saying is* _____ .

B. Active listening also involves CLARIFYING.

Clarifying involves asking questions to get more information.

Clarifying helps you hear more specifics about the situation and feelings.

Clarifying also lets the other person know you are interested in what he or she is saying.

- *So tell me what happened that got you so upset.*
- *How did you feel when that happened?*

C. Active listening often involves PERSONALIZING.

Personalizing involves offering a personal example of feeling the same thing or being in the same situation.

- *I think I know what you mean. I've been there too.*
- *I felt the same way when I lost my job. I think everyone does.*

Personalizing helps the other person feel less alone, and it implies that someone else has experienced this and has recovered from it.

Personalizing can be harmful if you talk too much about yourself and steal the spotlight from the person who needs it.

- *You think that was bad? Listen to what happened to me!*

D. Active listening does not mean cheering up, defending yourself, judging the person, or just repeating back exactly what was said.

- *All I ever do is the dirty work around here!*
- *Oh, come on, it's a hot day, you're just in a bad mood, don't worry about it.*

You can't trust anyone around this place!

- *Now, now, it's okay. It's all going to be better—I'll take care of it for you.*

I'm really worried that my family is going to be mad at me for dropping out of school.
- *You shouldn't feel that way.*

I keep trying to talk to you about how to handle the kids and you never listen to me!
- *I'm in charge! No more discussion!*

This place is really disgusting.
- *It sounds like you think this place is really disgusting.*

Some keys to being a GOOD ACTIVE LISTENER:
- Good eye contact, leaning slightly forward, reinforcing by nodding or paraphrasing, clarifying by asking questions
- Avoiding distractions
- Trying to really understand what the other person is really saying

COMMUNICATION ROADBLOCKS

◆ Handout

Adapted with permission from Koonin, M., Cabarcas, A., & Geffner, R. (2002). Women ending abusive/violent episodes respectfully (WEAVER) manual. San Diego CA: Family Violence and Sexual Assault Institute.

We often block communication by using these kinds of responses:
(Put a mark by any of these that you have ever used with your partner)

1. _____ Ordering/directing/commanding

    Don't talk about your mother like that.
    Stop complaining.

2. _____ Warning/threatening

    If you do that/you'll be sorry.
    I can dish it out too/you know!

3. _____ Moralizing/preaching/shoulds

    You shouldn't act like that.
    A real man would never treat a woman like that.

4. _____ Advising/giving solutions

    If you don't like it, you should just leave.

5. _____ Judging/criticizing/name-calling/labeling

    You are so stupid that you never get anything right!
    You will always be a loser.

6. _____ Reassuring/sympathizing/consoling

    You'll feel different tomorrow.
    Just forget it/it's no big deal.

7. _____ Interpreting/analyzing/diagnosing

    This is because of your unresolved issues with your father.

8. _____ Sarcasm/Humor

    Oh, you're going to start crying now?

Take a minute to think about the ones you have checked off. Is it possible that the use of these has messed up communication with someone important in your life?

SESSION 12 HOMEWORK #1

◆ Handout

Record three examples of your Active Listening responses over the next week.

1. Situation:

    You Said:

2. Situation:

    You Said:

3. Situation:

    You Said:

SESSION 12 HOMEWORK #2

◆ Handout

Also: Fill out the questionnaire below on the Love Languages Personal Profile in preparation for the next group session!

1. Go the web page for the Love Languages® Quiz at 5 Love Languages (https://www.5lovelanguages.com/profile/couples/).

2. Fill out the information to get started on the quiz.

3. Complete this quiz online (should take 5–10 minutes).

4. Print results indicating your Love Languages Personal Profile and bring it with you to the next group session.

THE FIVE LOVE LANGUAGES

◆ **Handout**

Adapted with permission from Chapman, G. (2015). The 5 Love Languages®: The secret to love that lasts. Chicago: Northfield Publishing.

1. If you really love someone, you find a way to love that person the way he really wants to be loved.

2. Sometimes (often!) love languages are mismatched. This does not have to be a major problem—as long as you recognize your partner's language and try to speak to him in that language. And, when you feel like you are not being loved, remember that your partner may be showing love in a different language.

3. As you think about these love languages, remember that you are identifying what is most important to you. You are *not* evaluating your partner's performance.

Physical Touch

This language isn't all about the bedroom. A person whose primary language is Physical Touch is, not surprisingly, very touchy. Hugs, pats on the back, holding hands, and thoughtful touches on the arm, shoulder, or face—they can all be ways to show excitement, concern, care, and love. Physical presence and accessibility are crucial, while neglect or abuse can be unforgivable and destructive. Physical touch fosters a sense of security and belonging in any relationship.

Quality Time

For Quality Time people, nothing says "I love you" like full, undivided attention. Being there for this type of person is critical, but really being there—with the TV off, fork and knife down, not texting, and all chores and tasks on standby—makes your significant other feel truly special and loved. Distractions, postponed dates, or the failure to listen can be especially hurtful. Quality Time also means sharing quality conversation and quality activities.

Words of Affirmation

Actions don't always speak louder than words. If this is your love language, unsolicited compliments mean the world to you. Hearing the words "I love you" is important—hearing the reasons behind that love sends your spirits skyward. Insults can leave you shattered and are not easily forgotten. Kind, encouraging, and positive words are truly life-giving.

Acts of Service

Can vacuuming the floors really be an expression of love? Absolutely! Anything you do to ease the burden of responsibilities weighing on an Acts of Service person will speak volumes. The words he or she most wants to hear are "Let me do that for you." Laziness, broken commitments, and making more work for them tell them that their feelings don't matter. Finding ways to serve speaks loud and clear.

Receiving Gifts

Don't mistake this love language for materialism; the receiver of gifts thrives on the love, thoughtfulness, and effort behind the gift. If you speak this language, the perfect gift or gesture shows that you are known, you are cared for, and you are prized above whatever was sacrificed to bring the gift to you. A missed birthday, anniversary, or a hasty, thoughtless gift would be disastrous—so would the absence of everyday gestures. Gifts are visual representations of love.

SESSION 13 HOMEWORK

Handout

Now fill out the Love Languages Quiz—this time from the perspective of your partner (or most recent partner). One way to do this is for your partner to actually fill it out, then discuss the results together. Or, if that is not possible, just fill this out as you believe your partner would answer it.

1. Go the web page for the Love Languages® Quiz at 5 Love Languages (https://www.5lovelanguages.com/profile/couples/).

2. Fill out the information to get started on the quiz.

3. Complete this quiz online (should take 5–10 minutes).

4. Print results indicating your Love Languages Personal Profile and bring it with you to the next group session.

FOUR HORSEMEN OF THE APOCALYPSE

◆ Handout

ACCUSATIONS (CRITICISM)

Complaints are expressed in a destructive manner, as an attack on the other person's character: *You're so thoughtless and self-centered!*

In a constructive complaint, the person states specifically what is upsetting her, and constructively criticizes the other person's action, not the person himself, saying how it made her feel.

CONTEMPT (DISGUST)

Contempt is usually expressed not just in the words themselves but also in a tone of voice and an angry expression. Rolling the eyes. A look of disgust.

What distinguishes contempt is the intention to insult and psychologically abuse the other person. When contempt begins to overwhelm the relationship, one person tends to forget entirely the other person's positive qualities, at least when feeling upset. She can't remember a single positive quality or act.

DEFENSIVENESS

Defensiveness is the fighting-back response. Here the person refuses to take in anything the other person is saying. It is one arm of the typical fight-or-flight response.

Defensiveness feels like an understandable reaction to feeling besieged—this is why it is so destructive. The victim doesn't see anything wrong with being defensive, even though this attitude escalates a conflict rather than leading to resolution. Defensive people *never* say, *Maybe you're right*, or *I see your point*, or *Yeah, I get it. I think I owe you an apology*.

STONEWALLING

Stonewalling is the ultimate defense. The stonewaller just goes blank and withdraws from the conversation. This sends a powerful message: icy distance, superiority, and distaste.

Don't confuse stonewalling with a time-out. A time-out communicates respect. The time-out message is that the person cares enough about the relationship to take special efforts not to cause any further damage. And there is a very clear contract that the discussion will continue at a future time.

EMOTIONAL ABUSE AND MIND GAMES

◆ Handout

As with physical abuse, repeated emotional abuse can have severe effects on the victim's sense of self and sense of reality. These mind games sometimes leave more lasting damage than physical abuse. The person on the receiving end—male or female—may question his or her reality, feel powerless, become overdependent, and so on. Here are some examples:

Coercion

- *I am going to kill myself if you leave me!*
- *I'm gonna take these kids right now and you'll never see them again!*
- *I'll get a doctor to say you're crazy and put you away!*

Put-Downs

- *You're just like your mother, a fat, brainless ass!*
- *You're just like your father, a lazy, bull-headed ass!*
- *My mother was right about you—you'll never amount to anything!*
- *How come a big, strong guy like you can't make more money around here?*
- *You're acting crazy.*
- *There you go again—crying like a big baby.*
- *Nobody's ever going to want you!*

Control

- *I want to know everywhere you've been in the last 24 hours!*
- *I know you go to that school just so you can try to pick up some girl!*
- *Your family just messes you up—I don't ever want you to talk to them again!*
- *You can't go out. I want you to stay right at home with me.*

Blaming

- *It's your fault my career is going nowhere.*
- *Nobody else has ever made me violent! You must be doing something to cause this!*

Entitlement

- *I don't care what you think about my gambling—it's my money and I'll do what I want!*
- *So what if I bought that car without discussing it with you?*

MAY NOT BE REPRODUCED WITHOUT PERMISSION

CONFLICT WITH RESPECT

Handout

Arguments can be a useful way to solve problems, or they can be never-ending battles that can increase tension and the risk of abuse. The central theme here, as always, is respect. Can you offer your partner respect even when you're upset? The following guidelines can make a difference:

DANGEROUS: THE NEGATIVE START-UP

Why am I the only one who ever does any cleaning up around here!
It may seem true at the moment, but . . .

- it is an exaggeration of the truth.
- it does not honor the positive qualities of your partner.
- it is usually communicated in a hostile tone of voice.

INSTEAD: RULES FOR A SOFTENED START-UP

I know you've been really busy with the kids, but I could really use some help getting the kitchen cleaned up.

- *Be concise.*
- *In the initial start-up complaint sentence, complain but don't blame.*
- *Start with something positive.*
- *Make statements that start with "I" instead of "you."*
- *Describe what is happening, but don't evaluate or judge.*
- *Talk clearly about what you need.*
- *Be polite.*
- *Express appreciation.*
- *Don't store things up.*
- *Restate your feelings in terms of the more vulnerable emotions.*

HOW TO AVOID UNFAIR BEHAVIOR (DISRESPECT)

- *Do not use name-calling or put-downs.*
- *Do not drag up old wounds from the past.*
- *Stay on track; do not go off in different directions.*
- *Do not threaten or intimidate.*
- *Do not assume that you will either win or lose this argument.*

- *Do not save up all your gripes to dump on your partner all at once.*
- *Be careful of mind-reading self-talk. Don't assume the most negative things about your partner. ASK!*
- *Do not deny the facts. Come clean.*
- *Do not gloat over a victory in getting your way.*
- *Do not sulk, ignore, pout, withdraw, or give your partner the silent treatment.*

SESSION 14 HOMEWORK

◆ Handout

Practice the softened start-up three times. Record the results.

---

1. My softened start-up statement:

Response from my partner:

---

2. My softened start-up statement:

Response from my partner:

---

3. My softened start-up statement:

Response from my partner:

THE ART OF APOLOGIES

◆ **Handout**

Apologies grease the wheels of most successful relationships. The art of delivering a sincere and well-timed apology is one that all of us should be very skilled at.

The obvious trigger situation for an apology is when you realize that you have done something that has hurt someone you care about. Even if your action was not intended to hurt or you were not aware of how it would affect the other person, an apology is still in order.

To apologize successfully, you need to have a solid platform of self-worth to stand on in order to not collapse into shame. The more self-worth you have, the more you can handle the ego blow of offering an apology—because admitting mistakes does not make you a doomed or despicable person. Just an imperfect one.

An effective apology requires four distinct elements to make it more likely to be well received (which is, after all, the point of the apology in the first place):

1. THE BASIC STATEMENT: "I'm sorry." No rationalizations, no excuses, no hedging. Just a simple statement that you are sorry and what you are sorry for having done. It could be big or very minor—it doesn't matter.

   Start by describing exactly what you did wrong, then just acknowledge that this was a mistake. Accept responsibility:

   — *I'm really sorry I started teasing you in front of your friends.*
   — *I feel terrible for having that affair and I am really, really sorry for how I have hurt you!*
   — *Sorry I forgot to make that bill payment.*

   Remember to get your *but* out of your apology: A *but* might sound like this: *I'm sorry I yelled at you, but you weren't listening to me.* Just stick with *I'm sorry I yelled at you.* Using *but* signals a rationalization, an excuse, and a focus on the other person's behaviors.

   While often your partner may have pieces to apologize for, a true apology only focuses on your behaviors. Take ownership of your part, find out how it impacted the other person, and begin to repair.

2. DEMONSTRATION OF EMPATHY: You need to make it as clear as possible that you really understand the pain or anxiety or mistrust that your actions have created in your partner: *I realize now how hurt you feel and how hard it is for you to trust me again. I get it now—or at least I'm trying to.*

   You need to make sure that you have listened to your partner's pain and that you clearly communicate the following message: *I want you to know that this is* not *going to slip out of my head.*

3. DEMONSTRATION OF INSIGHT: You need to offer the other person some evidence that you have learned something, or that there was some temporary circumstance that will not happen again, or at least that you will really be on guard against it the next time around:

   — *I think I was just feeling insecure, and this was some sort of way to make jokes and fit in! I won't let that happen again.*

— *There's no excuse—it had everything to do with me and feeling like I'm not getting enough attention. I wish there was some way I could go back in time and talk to you about what I've been going through instead of doing what I did!*
— *I was really rushing around last night, and I didn't pay attention. I'm going to start writing it in my appointment book to make sure I remember each month.*

"It's never enough to feel bad about an offense; **the hurt partner needs to hear reasons to feel safe in the future.**"—Steven Stosny, in Wachtel, E. (2019, March/April). Storm damage. *Psychotherapy Networker*, 61–64.

4. BEHAVIOR CHANGE: The proof is in the pudding. All the words and all the good intentions in the world don't mean a thing unless your partner sees, over time, that you have genuinely learned something from your mistake and that you are handling situations differently. Maybe not 100% perfectly, but definitely better. Remember that your partner cannot possibly feel secure until he or she has observed, over time, that you have changed. Obviously, the length of time that this takes is directly related to how serious the crime was.

CLASSIC APOLOGY MISTAKES

◆ Handout

1. Not being genuine. How do you like it when you hear *I'm sorry you feel that way* or *I'm sorry if that hurt your feelings*? Sometimes that might be okay, but most of the time this does not show sincere regret. In fact, it often makes your partner feel stupid for overreacting or being too sensitive. This usually does not get a passing grade as a genuine apology.

2. Crummy body language. Maybe the words are right, but there is no eye contact or even a hostile look. Or the tone of voice sounds sarcastic. This also fails the grade.

3. Waiting for the perfect moment. **It is never too late to apologize.** Some people wait for the perfect moment for an apology. This does not exist (although it's probably best not to do it in heavy traffic or when the baby is screaming). The perfect moment to apologize is the moment you realize you've done something wrong, or as soon as possible thereafter.

4. Getting defensive (see Nondefensive Listening below). Often we listen for the part of the criticisms or anger that we don't agree with, or some minor flaw in the person's story of what happened, or sometime when the other person treated us this way, or a reason the other person was oversensitive—anything to deflect from the simple responsibility of recognizing a mistake and apologizing for it.

5. Not listening carefully. Apologizing is much more than offering the words *I am sorry*. While these words mark the beginning, it is a process that can sometimes feel like a long-distance run. At the core of an honest and authentic apology is the ability to listen. You must be willing to sit with your partner's anger and pain. You need to stay there long enough to really grasp the injury and to validate the feelings.

6. Expecting immediate and total forgiveness. Remember Commandment 5: *We do not have control over any other person, but we do have control over ourselves*. All you can do is give it your best and most sincere shot. Your partner may never be able to forgive you, or at least it may take a while.

7. Apologizing too much. Some people apologize way too much, for the smallest things, or even when they haven't really done anything wrong. This is just plain irritating, and it's like crying wolf. The real and significant apologies will be weakened if trivial apologies distract attention from real issues.

SESSION 15 HOMEWORK #1

Handout

Identify three apologies to offer to your partner or children. Make the apology and record the response from the other person. If you are not in contact with any of them, identify three apologies you would make if you had the opportunity.

1. Apology from you:

    Response from partner or child:

2. Apology from you:

    Response from partner or child:

3. Apology from you:

    Response from partner or child:

SESSION 15 HOMEWORK #2

◆ Handout

Adapted with permission from Attached: The New Science Of Adult Attachment And How It Can Help You Find-And Keep-Love, *by Amir Levine, MD, and Rachel S. F. Heller, MA,, copyright ©️ 2010 by Amir Levine and Rachel Heller. Used by permission of Tarcher, an imprint of Penguin Publishing Group, a division of Penguin Random House LLC. All rights reserved.*

Fill out the "Which Attachment Style Am I?" questionnaire below and score in preparation for next session:

WHICH ATTACHMENT STYLE AM I? If TRUE, check white box. If FALSE, leave blank.	TRUE A	TRUE B	TRUE C
I often worry that my partner will stop loving me.			
I find it easy to be affectionate with my partner.			
I fear that once someone gets to know the real me, he/she won't like who I am.			
I find that I bounce back quickly after a breakup. It's weird how I can just put someone out of my mind.			
When I'm not involved in a relationship, I feel somewhat anxious and incomplete.			
I find it difficult to emotionally support my partner when he/she feels down.			
When my partner is away, I'm afraid that he/she might become interested in someone else.			
I feel comfortable depending on my romantic partner.			
My independence is more important to me than my relationships.			
I prefer not to share my innermost feelings with my partner.			
When I show my partner how I feel, I'm afraid he/she will not feel the same about me.			
I am generally satisfied with my romantic relationships.			
I don't feel the need to act out much in my romantic relationships.			
I think about my relationship a lot.			
I find it difficult to depend on a romantic partner.			
I tend to get very quickly attached to a romantic partner.			

WHICH ATTACHMENT STYLE AM I? If TRUE, check white box. If FALSE, leave blank.	TRUE A	TRUE B	TRUE C
I have little difficulty expressing my needs to my partner.			
I sometimes feel angry or annoyed with my partner without knowing why.			
I am very sensitive to my partner's moods.			
I believe most people are essentially honest and dependable.			
I prefer casual sex with uncommitted partners to intimate sex with one person.			
I'm comfortable sharing my personal thoughts and feelings with my partner.			
I worry that if my partner leaves me, I might never find someone else.			
It makes me nervous when my partner gets too close.			
During a conflict, I tend to impulsively do or say things I later regret, rather than being able to reason about things.			
An argument with my partner doesn't usually cause me to question our entire relationship.			
My partners often want me to be more intimate than I feel comfortable being.			
I worry that I am not attractive enough.			
Sometimes people see me as boring because I create little drama in a relationship.			
I miss my partner when we're apart, but then when we're together I feel the need to escape.			
When I disagree with someone, I feel comfortable expressing my feelings.			
I hate that other people depend on me.			
If I notice that someone I'm interested in is checking out other people, I don't let it faze me. I might feel a pang of jealousy, but it's fleeting.			
If I notice that someone I'm interested in is checking out other people, I feel relieved—it means that he/she's not looking to make things exclusive.			
If I notice that someone I'm interested in is checking out other people, it makes me feel depressed.			
If someone I've been dating begins to act cold and distant, I may wonder what's happened, but I know it's probably not about me.			

If someone I've been dating begins to act cold and distant, I'll probably be indifferent; I might even be relieved.			
If someone I've been dating begins to act cold and distant, I'll worry that I've done something wrong.			
If my partner was to break up with me, I'd try my best to show him/her what he/she is missing (a little jealousy can't hurt).			
If someone I've been dating for several months tells me they want to stop seeing me, I'd feel hurt at first, but I'd get over it.			
Sometimes when I get what I want in a relationship, I'm not sure what I want anymore.			
I won't have much of a problem staying in touch with my ex (strictly platonic)—after all, we have a lot in common.			

Add up all your checked boxes in Column A: ____ Column B: ____ Column C: ____
Scoring Key: The more statements that you check in a category, the more you will display characteristics of the corresponding attachment style.

Category A—Anxious:

- You love to be very close to your partner and have the capacity for great intimacy. You often fear, however, that your partner does not wish to be as close as you would like him to be.
- Relationships tend to consume a large part of your emotional energy.
- You tend to be very sensitive to small fluctuations in your partner's moods and actions, and you sometimes take his behavior too personally.
- You experience a lot of negative emotions within the relationship and get easily upset. As a result, you tend to act out and say things you later regret.
- If the other person provides a lot of security and reassurance, however, you are able to let go of your preoccupation and feel contented.

Category B—Secure:

- Being warm and loving in a relationship comes naturally to you.
- You enjoy being intimate without becoming overly worried about your relationships. You take things in stride when it comes to romance and don't get easily upset over relationship matters.
- You effectively communicate your needs and feelings to your partner and are strong at reading his emotional cues and responding to them.
- You share your successes and problems with your partner, and you are able to be there in times of need.

Category C—Avoidant:

- It is very important for you to maintain your independence and self-sufficiency, and you often prefer autonomy to intimate relationships.

- Even though you do want to be close to others, you feel uncomfortable with too much closeness and tend to keep your partner at arm's length.

- You don't spend much time worrying about your romantic relationships or about being rejected.

- You tend not to open up to your partner, and he often complains that you are emotionally distant.

- In relationships, you are often on high alert for any signs of control or impingement on your territory by your partner.

CAN I COUNT ON YOU?

Handout

Everyone walks around with doubts and insecurities about their intimate relationships. Here's a list of typical worries that people carry around. Can you count on positive answers to these questions in your relationship? Can your partner count on positive answers about you?

- *Will I be physically safe?*
- *Do I really matter to you enough that you'll put me first when it really counts—before your job, before your friends, even before your family?*
- *Can I count on you to give me space when I need it?*
- *Do I have to worry about you abandoning me?*
- *Do I have to worry about competing with someone else?*
- *Can I trust you not to hurt or humiliate me?*
- *Do I have to worry about your threats?*
- *Can I count on the fact that I really know you?*
- *Are you really paying attention to who I am and not who you imagine or want me to be? Can I be myself with you?*
- *Can I count on you to really act like an adult?*
- *Do you really value me, cherish me? Can I count on you to consistently let me know how important I am to you?*

SECURE COMMUNICATION

◆ Handout

SITUATION	INSECURE ATTACHMENT RESPONSE	EFFECTIVE COMMUNICATION
He's very busy at work and you hardly get to see him.	Call him every couple of hours to make sure you're on his mind.	Tell him you miss him and are having a hard time adjusting to his new work schedule, even though you understand that it's temporary.
He doesn't really listen to you when you're talking, which makes you feel unimportant and misunderstood.	Get up in the middle of the conversation and go to another room (hoping he will follow you and apologize).	Make it clear that it's not enough that he listens without responding. Emphasize that you value his opinion above anyone's and it's important to you to know what he thinks.
She talks about her ex-girlfriend, which makes you feel insecure.	Tell her it's pathetic that he's still talking about her ex, or . . . Bring up other women you went out with to let her know how bad it feels.	Let her know that conversations about her ex make you feel inadequate and unsure of where you stand, that you need to feel secure in order to be happy with someone.
He always changes plans at the last minute.	Do the same thing to him so eventually he'll learn how it feels.	Explain that you feel unsettled not being able to count on plans with him and that it's better for you to at least have a ballpark schedule most of the time.

It's important to remember that even with effective communication, some problems won't be solved immediately. What's vital is your partner's response—whether he is concerned about your well-being, has your best interest in mind, and is willing to work on things.

From Levine, A., & Heller, R. (2010). Attached. London: Rodale.

SESSION 16 HOMEWORK

◆ Handout

Now fill out the Which Attachment Style Am I? questionnaire—this time from the perspective of your partner (or most recent partner). One way is for your partner to actually fill it out, then discuss the results together. Or, if that is not possible, just fill this out as you believe your partner would answer it. See if it helps you understand your partner better and why certain situations activate your partner's fears.

WHICH ATTACHMENT STYLE AM I? If TRUE, check white box. If FALSE, leave blank.	TRUE A	TRUE B	TRUE C
I often worry that my partner will stop loving me.			
I find it easy to be affectionate with my partner.			
I fear that once someone gets to know the real me, he/she won't like who I am.			
I find that I bounce back quickly after a breakup. It's weird how I can just put someone out of my mind.			
When I'm not involved in a relationship, I feel somewhat anxious and incomplete.			
I find it difficult to emotionally support my partner when he/she feels down.			
When my partner is away, I'm afraid that he/she might become interested in someone else.			
I feel comfortable depending on my romantic partner.			
My independence is more important to me than my relationships.			
I prefer not to share my innermost feelings with my partner.			
When I show my partner how I feel, I'm afraid he/she will not feel the same about me.			
I am generally satisfied with my romantic relationships.			
I don't feel the need to act out much in my romantic relationships.			
I think about my relationship a lot.			
I find it difficult to depend on a romantic partner.			
I tend to get very quickly attached to a romantic partner.			

WHICH ATTACHMENT STYLE AM I? If TRUE, check white box. If FALSE, leave blank	TRUE A	TRUE B	TRUE C
I have little difficulty expressing my needs to my partner.			
I sometimes feel angry or annoyed with my partner without knowing why.			
I am very sensitive to my partner's moods.			
I believe most people are essentially honest and dependable.			
I prefer casual sex with uncommitted partners to intimate sex with one person.			
I'm comfortable sharing my personal thoughts and feelings with my partner.			
I worry that if my partner leaves me, I might never find someone else.			
It makes me nervous when my partner gets too close.			
During a conflict, I tend to impulsively do or say things I later regret, rather than being able to reason about things.			
An argument with my partner doesn't usually cause me to question our entire relationship.			
My partners often want me to be more intimate than I feel comfortable being.			
I worry that I am not attractive enough.			
Sometimes people see me as boring because I create little drama in a relationship.			
I miss my partner when we're apart, but then when we're together I feel the need to escape.			
When I disagree with someone, I feel comfortable expressing my feelings.			
I hate that other people depend on me.			
If I notice that someone I'm interested in is checking out other people, I don't let it faze me. I might feel a pang of jealousy, but it's fleeting.			
If I notice that someone I'm interested in is checking out other people, I feel relieved—it means that he/she's not looking to make things exclusive.			
If I notice that someone I'm interested in is checking out other people, it makes me feel depressed.			
If someone I've been dating begins to act cold and distant, I may wonder what's happened, but I know it's probably not about me.			
If someone I've been dating begins to act cold and distant, I'll probably be indifferent; I might even be relieved.			

If someone I've been dating begins to act cold and distant, I'll worry that I've done something wrong.			
If my partner was to break up with me, I'd try my best to show him/her what he/she is missing (a little jealousy can't hurt).			
If someone I've been dating for several months tells me they want to stop seeing me, I'd feel hurt at first, but I'd get over it.			
Sometimes when I get what I want in a relationship, I'm not sure what I want anymore.			
I won't have much of a problem staying in touch with my ex (strictly platonic)—after all, we have a lot in common.			

Add up all your checked boxes in Column A: ____ Column B: ____ Column C: ____

Scoring Key: The more statements that you check in a category, the more you will display characteristics of the corresponding attachment style.

Category A—Anxious:

- You love to be very close to your partner and have the capacity for great intimacy. You often fear, however, that your partner does not wish to be as close as you would like her to be.
- Relationships tend to consume a large part of your emotional energy.
- You tend to be very sensitive to small fluctuations in your partner's moods and actions, and you sometimes take her behavior too personally.
- You experience a lot of negative emotions within the relationship and get easily upset. As a result, you tend to act out and say things you later regret.
- If the other person provides a lot of security and reassurance, however, you are able to let go of your preoccupation and feel contented.

Category B—Secure:

- Being warm and loving in a relationship comes naturally to you.
- You enjoy being intimate without becoming overly worried about your relationships. You take things in stride when it comes to romance and don't get easily upset over relationship matters.
- You effectively communicate your needs and feelings to your partner and are strong at reading her emotional cues and responding to them.
- You share your successes and problems with your partner, and you are able to be there in times of need.

Category C—Avoidant:

- It is very important for you to maintain your independence and self-sufficiency and you often prefer autonomy to intimate relationships.

- Even though you do want to be close to others, you feel uncomfortable with too much closeness and tend to keep your partner at arm's length.
- You don't spend much time worrying about your romantic relationships or about being rejected.
- You tend not to open up to your partner and they often complain that you are emotionally distant.
- In relationships, you are often on high alert for any signs of control or impingement on your territory by your partner.

RELATIONSHIP RESPECT CONTRACT

◆ **Handout**

We recognize that our relationship will only have a chance to be successful if all of these guidelines are followed:

1. No incidents of direct physical abuse or violence.
2. No direct or implied threats of physical abuse or violence (to self, other, or property).
3. No direct or implied threats to behave in a way that would be extremely harmful to the other person (such as exposing personal secrets).
4. No physical restrictions on either party's freedom of movement.
5. No property destruction as an expression of aggression.
6. No threats to leave the relationship (except for temporary time-outs to defuse tension).
7. No pattern of extreme verbal put-downs, or character assassinations, or other humiliating acts.
8. No acts of infidelity or behaviors that suggest infidelity.
9. No pattern of lying or deception.
10. No pattern of abusing alcohol or drugs.

Other: _____

Both parties also agree to make all reasonable efforts to focus on building the positive aspects of the relationship rather than just complaining about the bad behavior of the other party.

_____   _____
Name   Date

_____   _____
Name   Date

CONTRACT VIOLATIONS

◆ Handout

Identify the ways this Relationship Respect Contract has been broken in the past, by you and by your partner.

CONTRACT ITEMS	VIOLATED IN PAST, SELF (YES/NO)?	VIOLATED IN PAST, PARTNER (YES/NO)?
1. No incidents of direct physical abuse or violence.		
2. No direct or implied threats of physical abuse or violence (to self, other, or property).		
3. No direct or implied threats to behave in a way that would be extremely harmful to the other person (such as exposing personal secrets).		
4. No physical restrictions on either party's freedom of movement.		
5. No property destruction as an expression of aggression.		
6. No threats to leave the relationship (except for temporary time-outs to defuse tension).		
7. No pattern of extreme verbal put-downs, or character assassinations, or other humiliating acts.		
8. No acts of infidelity or behaviors that suggest infidelity.		
9. No pattern of lying or deception.		
10. No pattern of abusing alcohol or drugs.		

SESSION 17 HOMEWORK

◆ Handout

Complete the Contract Violations chart below.

Then review the Relationship Respect Contract with your partner. Together, identify the ways this contract has been broken in the past, and see if you can both commit to at least *trying* to make sure the contract is honored by both parties in the future. IF YOU CAN, YOU SHOULD BOTH SIGN IT.

If you are no longer together or your partner is otherwise unavailable, write three additional items that you would include on your own personal Relationship Respect Contract for future relationships:

1.

2.

3.

CONTRACT ITEMS	VIOLATED IN PAST, SELF (YES/NO)?	VIOLATED IN PAST, PARTNER (YES/NO)?
1. No incidents of direct physical abuse or violence.		
2. No direct or implied threats of physical abuse or violence (to self, other, or property).		
3. No direct or implied threats to behave in a way that would be extremely harmful to the other person (such as exposing personal secrets).		
4. No physical restrictions on either party's freedom of movement.		

CONTRACT ITEMS	VIOLATED IN PAST, SELF (YES/NO)?	VIOLATED IN PAST, PARTNER (YES/NO)?
5. No property destruction as an expression of aggression.		
6. No threats to leave the relationship (except for temporary time-outs to defuse tension).		
7. No pattern of extreme verbal put-downs, or character assassinations, or other humiliating acts.		
8. No acts of infidelity or behaviors that suggest infidelity.		
9. No pattern of lying or deception.		
10. No pattern of abusing alcohol or drugs.		

WHY MEN KEEP THEIR MOUTHS SHUT ABOUT DOMESTIC VIOLENCE

♦ **Handout**

1. Men are afraid of being identified as a wimp and being ridiculed:

   Your GIRLFRIEND did this to you?? What's wrong with you?

2. Just like women, men don't want to face shame from others:

   Why did you pick a partner like that? What's wrong with you?
   Why did you put up with this for so long? What's wrong with you?

3. Men are afraid they will be identified as the cause of her violence:

   Come on, you MUST have done something to make her do this!

4. Men are not confident that they will be able to find community resources to support them: the police, court systems, or counselors might not believe them, shelters and victims' services for men are rarely available, and so on.

5. Just like women, men may fear that if they disclose the abuse or end the relationship, their partner might become more abusive and/or take the children.

6. And, just like women, abused men often don't report or leave because they still love their wives, they don't want to break up their family, they made a commitment to make the marriage work, they don't really want their partner to suffer the consequences and humiliation of the legal system—and they cannot tolerate the idea that they have somehow failed in their marriage.

SESSION 18 HOMEWORK

◆ Handout

Write one paragraph (at least 100 words) as if you are your husband or partner. The subject is "Sometimes I Don't Trust My Husband (or Partner) Because . . ."

SEXUAL PUT-DOWNS AND MIND GAMES

Handout

Sex can be, and should be, a wonderful aspect of a loving relationship. But often sexual messages are used in a way to hurt, retaliate, or control. If you can, try to be honest with yourself about which of these you may have used at some point in your relationships.

PUT-DOWNS

- Making jokes about men in your partner's presence
- Checking out other men in his presence
- Making sexual put-down jokes
- Comparing her body to other women or to pictures in magazines
- Criticizing his sexual performance
- Blaming your partner if you don't feel satisfied with sex

MIND GAMES

- Telling your partner that agreeing to sex is the only way they can prove they have been faithful or that they still love you
- Revealing intimate details about your partner to others
- Withholding sex and affection only to gain control over your partner
- Engaging in sexual affairs

GENDER PRESSURE

- *Real men should want it all the time.*
- *I owe sex to my partner whenever they want it.*

ABOUT SEX

◆ Handout

Adapted with permission from Koonin, M., Cabarcas, A., & Geffner, R. (2002). Women ending abusive/violent episodes respectfully (WEAVER) manual. San Diego CA: Family Violence and Sexual Assault Institute.

Sex has different meanings to each person. Some people view sex as a way to connect with another individual on a more intimate level. Some view sex as an extension of their love. Others may view sex as an outlet for stress and tension. The following is meant to help you clarify *your* definition of sex, and your values, feelings, and expectations when you are sexually intimate with someone.

I feel attractive to my partner when . . .

When my partner rejects me sexually, I (include feelings and actions) . . .

When I don't feel like being sexually intimate, I . . .

After having sex, I feel . . .

I think masturbation is . . .

A time I regret having sex (include why) . . .

A time I used sex to get what I wanted was . . .

I feel used sexually when . . .

Sex after an argument is . . .

Refusing sex to punish a partner is . . .

It is okay/not okay for me to cheat sexually on my partner because . . .

A person in a relationship should/should not flirt (include why) . . .

I think that men think sex is . . .

What I like most about sex with my partner is . . .

What I like least about sex with my partner is . . .

If I want to have sex and my partner doesn't, I usually . . .

SESSION 19 HOMEWORK

Handout

Based on your own life experience, prepare three messages or words of advice you would want to pass on to your daughter about how to handle sex in a meaningful relationship.

1.

2.

3.

WHO DECIDES?

Handout

Adapted with permission from Pence, E., & Paymar, M. (1993). Education groups for men who batter: The Duluth model. New York: Springer.

Check below whether you think an item should be your decision, your partner's decision, or open to negotiation. Remember that there are no right or wrong answers here—as long as both partners agree about the decision-making process.

	Your decision	Mostly yours	Joint decision	Mostly your partner's	Partner's decision
1. Which friends can your partner spend time with?					
2. Which friends can you spend time with?					
3. Can your partner drink on certain occasions?					
4. Can you drink on certain occasions?					
5. Who decides on a sitter for the children?					
6. Will your partner get a job/go to school?					
7. Will you get a job/go to school?					

	Your decision	Mostly yours	Joint decision	Mostly your partner's	Partner's decision
8. How will your partner dress when he or she leaves the house?					
9. How will you dress when you leave the house?					
10. How will the children be disciplined?					
11. What is your paycheck spent on?					
12. What is your partner's paycheck spent on?					

RULES AND ROLES: SPOKEN AND UNSPOKEN

Handout

Every relationship has rules and roles. When both people understand the rules—and agree to them—relationships work. When the rules are not clear—or when they are clear but violated—relationships suffer.

CATEGORY #1: DEAL-BREAKER RULES

These are rules that are usually clear to both parties, like . . .

- *It's not okay to cheat on me.*
- *I need you to be there for me when I am sick or distressed.*
- *It would be horrible if either of us tried to turn the kids against the other parent.*

CATEGORY #2: ASSUMED EXPECTATIONS

These are rules or expectations that we may have learned in our families or from previous relationships that we just assume everybody else would have, like . . .

- *Friday night is okay to spend with my friends, but Saturday night we always have to be together.*
- *We always have to eat dinner as a family.*
- *Christmas Eve is for a big dinner; Christmas Day is just for opening presents and hanging out.*

CATEGORY #3: RELATIONSHIP ROLES

These are expectations about the roles each of you are supposed to play in your relationship, like . . .

- *People should never raise their voice in a discussion.*
- *It's not okay for a man to cry.*
- *I need you to drop everything and talk to me when I need attention.*

SESSION 20 HOMEWORK

Handout

Review the Rules and Roles handout. Based on these categories, identify one example of each category from your relationship:

1. What is one of the DEAL-BREAKER RULES or expectations in your relationship?

2. Now that you think about it, what is one of your ASSUMED RULES that you think *everybody* should understand?

3. What are some RELATIONSHIP ROLE issues that have been incompatible or caused conflict for you and your partner?

QUESTIONS FOR KIDS

Handout

In this exercise, group members take turns role-playing, being the child in their house who has witnessed violence. Other group members interview these "kids" about their experiences.

1. What kinds of things do your mom and dad fight about?

2. What happens when your mom or dad gets angry or your parents fight? Can you describe any fights between your parents that you saw yourself? What did you see or hear during the fight? What was it like for you afterward (e.g., did you see your parents' injuries or the house torn apart)? What were your reactions?

3. What do you do if your parents push, shove, or hit each other? Do you leave the room or go outside?

4. Can you describe any fights between your parents in which you were caught in the middle, or when you tried to stop them? What happened?

5. Do they ever fight about you? How does this make you feel (scared, confused, sad, mad)?

6. Do you talk to anybody about this?

7. How do you handle your feelings since this has happened? Do you ever feel like hurting yourself or anyone else?

8. In an emergency for you or your parents, who would you call? Where could you go?

SESSION 21 HOMEWORK

Handout

Complete the following Kid Stories exercise and bring it for group review next session.

1. You are an 8-year-old girl, and you really like playing video games more than anything else. Your dad has been getting drunk lately. He comes home and hits your mom, and he breaks things after he thinks the kids have gone to sleep. Your older sister has started using drugs and running away. One day after school, your mom says you're all going to be moving away from your dad, with her, to another town across the state, near your aunt and uncle. Your mom tells you that she can't trust your dad anymore and that you kids might be the next to get hurt. You've never seen your dad hit your sister, and he's never hit you.

   How would you feel when you heard about your mom's plans?

   How would you feel toward her?

   How would you feel toward your father?

2. You are a 10-year-old girl who's been really screwing up at school lately. Your dad is constantly on your case; it seems like nothing you do is right. You know your mom has been spending a lot of money, and he is always yelling at her about it. One time he locked her out of the house, and she had to stay outside in the rain until you snuck around the back to let her in. She yells right back at him, calling him bad names. Sometimes she even throws things at him and you can hear things breaking. You and your mom have left a couple of times for a few days, but she always comes back. It's hard for you to sleep. You want this to stop, and you ask if you can live with somebody else for a while.

   How would you feel toward your mother?

   How would you feel toward your father?

ACCOUNTABILITY ASSUMPTION

◆ Handout

We are making an assumption here—that all of you want the best in your relationship and do not want to be in an abusive or destructive relationship. But something seems to come along and bring out behaviors in you that you thought you would never do.

We want to help you figure out what you have told yourself at those times when you have acted aggressively that somehow made it seem right or fair at the time.

When you figure this out, you become more powerful. And you become more fully accountable for your own actions. When you know what to look for, you are more likely to act like the woman you really want to be.

ACCOUNTABILITY DEFENSES

Handout

Most people who behave destructively toward their partner find a way to justify it in their own minds. Even though they do not usually believe in being abusive toward a family member or partner, in certain situations they make an exception.

Then, afterward, they figure out some way to make it okay, rather than simply saying the obvious: I blew it. I crossed over a line, and it's nobody's fault but my own.

Here are some typical examples.

NO BIG DEAL: I wasn't violent; all I did was slap him.

INTENTION: I didn't mean to hurt him—I just wanted him to understand!

SELF-EXPRESSION: It was my turn to let him know what I've been going through!

INTOXICATION/LOSS OF CONTROL: I was drunk; what can I say?/I just flipped out; I didn't even know what I was doing.

PROJECTION OF BLAME: It's his fault; if he hadn't pushed me, or nagged me, or spent too much money . . .

ACCOUNTABILITY STATEMENT

◆ Handout

Adapted with permission from Pence, E., & Paymar, M. (1993). Education groups for men who batter: The Duluth model. New York: Springer.

To be accountable means to acknowledge and take responsibility for one's actions. This handout will help you acknowledge destructive behavior in relationships. Although such behavior does not always turn into physical abuse, practically everyone—in almost *all* emotionally intimate relationships—behaves destructively at times. This is an opportunity to recognize past mistakes and demonstrate a desire to change them.

As you fill out this form, remember Commandment #1: *We are all 100% responsible for our own actions*. You will not be turning this in, but we will use your response in discussion.

We are not asking you to admit to something that you did not do, or to take responsibility for something that someone else has done.

I have acted in the following destructive ways toward my partner. (Circle each)

Verbal Abuse	Controlling Partner	Intimidation	Mind Games
Property Destruction	Manipulating Kids	Threats	Forced Sex
Put-Downs	Stalking	Monitoring Mail/Phones	Sexual Put-Downs
Isolation of Partner	Controlling Money	Ignoring/ Withdraw	Affairs
Physical Restraint	Pushing	Slapping	Kicking
Throwing Things	Choking	Use of Weapons	Other

Other: _____

- I take responsibility for these destructive behaviors. My behavior was not *caused* by my partner. I had a choice.

- I have used the following to rationalize my destructive behaviors in this relationship (e.g., alcohol, stress, anger, "he was criticizing me," etc.):

    1. _____
    2. _____
    3. _____

- I recognize that my partner may be distrustful, intimidated, and fearful of me because of these behaviors.

SESSION 22 HOMEWORK #1

Handout

Over the next week, pay attention to your self-talk and behaviors. Identify two examples in which you blamed someone else for your feelings or behaviors. You may use examples from the past if none occur to you this week.

1.

2.

SESSION 22 HOMEWORK #2

Handout

Fill out the MAST questionnaire below and score in preparation for next session.

MICHIGAN ALCOHOL SCREENING TEST (MAST)

1. Do you feel like a normal drinker? ("normal" = drink as much as or less than most people)
   Circle Answer: YES   NO

2. Have you ever awakened the morning after some drinking the night before and found that you could not remember part of the evening?
   Circle Answer: YES   NO

3. Does any near relative or close friend ever worry or complain about your drinking?
   Circle Answer: YES   NO

4. Can you stop drinking without difficulty after one or two drinks?
   Circle Answer: YES   NO

5. Do you ever feel guilty about your drinking?
   Circle Answer: YES   NO

6. Have you ever attended a meeting of Alcoholics Anonymous (AA)?
   Circle Answer: YES   NO

7. Have you ever gotten into physical fights when drinking?
   Circle Answer: YES   NO

8. Has drinking ever created problems between you and a near relative or close friend?
   Circle Answer: YES   NO

9. Has any family member or close friend gone to anyone for help about your drinking?
   Circle Answer: YES   NO

10. Have you ever lost friends because of your drinking?
    Circle Answer: YES   NO

11. Have you ever gotten into trouble at work because of drinking?
    Circle Answer: YES   NO

12. Have you ever lost a job because of your drinking?

Circle Answer: YES   NO

13. Have you ever neglected your obligations, your family, or your work for two or more days in a row because you were drinking?

Circle Answer: YES   NO

14. Do you drink before noon fairly often?

Circle Answer: YES   NO

15. Have you ever been told you have liver trouble such as cirrhosis?

Circle Answer: YES   NO

16. After heavy drinking have you ever had delirium tremens (DTs), severe shaking, or visual or auditory (hearing) hallucinations?

Circle Answer: YES   NO

17. Have you ever gone to anyone for help about your drinking?

Circle Answer: YES   NO

18. Have you ever been hospitalized because of your drinking?

Circle Answer: YES   NO

19. Has your drinking ever resulted in you being hospitalized in a psychiatric ward?

Circle Answer: YES   NO

20. Have you ever gone to any doctor, social worker, clergyperson, or mental health clinic for help with any emotional problem in which drinking was part of the problem?

Circle Answer: YES   NO

21. Have you been arrested more than once for driving under the influence of alcohol?

Circle Answer: YES   NO

22. Have you ever been arrested, even for a few hours because of other behavior while drinking?

Circle Answer: YES   NO

Please score one point if you answered the following:

1. No
2. Yes
3. Yes
4. No
5. Yes
6. Yes
7.–22. Yes

Add up the scores and compare to the following score card:

0–2 = No apparent problem
3–5 = Early or middle problem drinker
6 or more = Problem drinker

I REALLY DIDN'T MEAN TO DO IT . . . I WAS DRUNK

Handout

Some people who hurt the ones they love have problems with alcohol. Some also have problems with other drugs, like pot, crack, and cocaine. Ours is a culture that often encourages the abuse of alcohol and the display of aggression under this influence. People under the influence sometimes do things impulsively they may not ordinarily do, and their judgment and control are impaired.

This session is about taking responsibility for all of your decisions and actions, including using substances.

People use chemicals for many different reasons. On the questionnaires that follow, think about the reasons you use alcohol or drugs. Then identify whether alcohol or other drugs impair your judgment or cause you to become aggressive.

And—ask yourself these questions as you think about the ways drugs or alcohol may be affecting your relationship problems:

- *Have you ever done something while under the influenced that you regretted afterward?*
- *Have you ever become more abusive or aggressive when using alcohol or drugs?*
- *Have you missed work/school due to your use?*
- *Have you made most of your bad choices while under the influence?*
- *Have you ever tried to cut back on your drinking or drug use?*
- *Has anyone ever been annoyed about your drinking or told you that you have a substance problem?*
- *Have you ever experienced memory lapses or blackouts?*

Any "yes" answers indicate that alcohol or drug use has probably impaired your ability to be fully in control of your life. Remember the 100% rule regarding responsibility. Alcohol and drug problems are usually progressive—without help, they get worse. Can you really be 100% committed to being in control of your life and still continue to abuse alcohol or drugs?

WHY DO WE CARE? THE RELATIONSHIP BETWEEN SUBSTANCE ABUSE AND INTIMATE PARTNER VIOLENCE

Handout

- 60% of domestic violence incidents involve perpetrators who are drinking.

- The likelihood of aggression is eight times higher on days when the perpetrator was drinking alcohol.

- Binge drinking is tied especially closely with partner abuse. Binge drinking is defined as the consumption of five or more standard drinks in one sitting, at least once in the preceding 30 days. Individuals who engage in binge drinking are five times as likely to have interpersonal conflicts with their partner and engage in aggressive behavior.

- Alcohol intoxication can lead to negative feelings of depression, helplessness, and hopelessness. Being depressed significantly increases the likelihood of IPV.

- Over 50% of alcoholics have been violent to a partner in the year before beginning alcoholism treatment.

Information provided by Donald Meichenbaum, PhD.

WHY DO I USE?

Handout

Think about the reasons that you use (or abuse) alcohol or other substances. Even if your use does not cause many problems in your life, it still serves some purpose. Check off on the list below the different reasons for your use of alcohol or other substances. We will discuss these in the next group session.

_____ To relax

_____ To feel more at ease in social situations

_____ Just because it tastes good

_____ Because my friends expect me to

_____ To have fun

_____ To avoid other people

_____ To feel more relaxed about having sex

_____ To avoid bad feelings (anger, depression, anxiety, loneliness, etc.)

_____ To have an excuse for getting rowdy

_____ To feel better about myself

_____ To stop worrying about problems

_____ To get a little buzzed

_____ To get really drunk

_____ To go to sleep

SESSION 23 HOMEWORK

Handout

Describe one time when you really regretted something you said or did under the influence that has been damaging to your relationship or your family (100 words):

STAKE IN CONFORMITY

Handout

One thing that stops people from crossing the line into violent behavior is a fear of losing something important.

But in order to fear loss, people must feel like they actually have something to lose. Research shows that arrest only works for people with something to lose by being arrested. People arrested for domestic violence with high levels of Stake in Conformity are less likely to assault their partners again after being arrested.

The higher your score, the greater the likelihood that you have a high Stake in Conformity and are less likely to commit any future acts of violence or aggression.

POTENTIAL LOSSES: How painful would it be if, because of your domestic violence, you (10 extremely painful, 0 not painful):

1. Lost your job _____

2. Lost your relationship _____

3. Lost access to your children _____

4. Served time in jail _____

5. Had to face your parents and other family members _____

6. Had to face your employer and coworkers _____

7. Had to face your friends _____

8. Had to face your church or religious group _____

SCREW YOU!

◆ Handout

Adapted with permission from Real, T., & Johnson, S. (2012). Confrontation in couples therapy—Who needs it? Psychotherapy Networker, 36(2), 46–61.

This is a description of a counseling session with a woman who described herself as a "rage-aholic." She would go off on her husband in wild verbal rages (never quite physical) in front of their kids, saying really insulting and damaging things that left everyone feeling wounded and scared.

She hated herself afterward and was seeking help to get more self-control. Here's how the counseling session went:

Counselor: *You have to stop doing this.*

She said, as most ragers do: *It comes upon me too quickly. I can't.*

Then the counselor made a strategic move: *Okay, here's what I want you to do. Do you have pictures of your kids?*

She got out her phone and showed him some pictures.

Counselor: *Okay, you have my permission to rage at your husband in front of your kids. But before you do that, I want you to look at some family photos of your kids and look into their eyes and say, "I know what I'm about to do is going to cause you deep and permanent harm, but right now, my anger is more important to me than you are, so screw you."*

He put his arm around her shoulder and said: *Let's practice that. Hold up the pictures, and say . . .*

She burst into tears: *I can't say that to my children.*

He said: *No, but you* are *saying that to your children. You're saying that each time you scream at their father in front of them. All I want you to do is say it out loud and own it.*

Then she said: *I'll never rage at my husband again for the rest of my life.*

SESSION 24 HOMEWORK #1

◆ **Handout**

Identify eight things that you stand to lose if you become abusive or violent with your partner again. The more of these you can come up with, the greater your Stake in Conformity.

1.

2.

3.

4.

5.

6.

7.

8.

SESSION 24 HOMEWORK #2

Handout (to come in *Handouts & Homework*)

Fill out the Safe at Home Questionnaire, Revised below and score in preparation for next session.

SAFE AT HOME QUESTIONNAIRE, REVISED

Instructions: Please circle the number that BEST describes how much you agree or disagree with each statement listed below.

ITEM #	ITEM STATEMENT	I Strongly Agree	I Agree	I Don't Agree or Disagree	I Disagree	I Strongly Disagree
1-C	The last time I lost control of myself, I realized that I have a problem.	1	2	3	4	5
2-M	I do not believe that I will return to my old ways of losing control.	1	2	3	4	5
3-P/A	I try to listen carefully to others so that I don't get into conflicts anymore.	1	2	3	4	5
4-C	It feels good to finally face how I've been messing up my life.	1	2	3	4	5
5-P	It's no big deal if I lose my temper from time to time.	1	2	3	4	5
6-P/A	I handle it safely when people get angry with me.	1	2	3	4	5
7-*	Sometimes I find that it is still very hard for me to avoid my old ways of treating my partner.	1	2	3	4	5
8-*	I have a problem with losing control of myself.	1	2	3	4	5
9-C	I want to do something about my problem with conflict.	1	2	3	4	5
10-C	I want help with my temper.	1	2	3	4	5
11-P	I'll come to groups but I won't talk.	1	2	3	4	5

ITEM #	ITEM STATEMENT	I Strongly Agree	I Agree	I Don't Agree or Disagree	I Disagree	I Strongly Disagree
12-P/A	I am actively keeping my cool when my partner(s) and I have conflicts.	1	2	3	4	5
13-C	I need to change before it's too late.	1	2	3	4	5
14-P	There's nothing wrong with the way I handle situations but I get into trouble for it anyway.	1	2	3	4	5
15-P/A	Even though I get angry I know ways to avoid losing control of myself.	1	2	3	4	5
16-M	I really am different now than I was when conflicts were a problem for me.	1	2	3	4	5
17-C	I guess I need help with the way I handle things.	1	2	3	4	5
18-P	It'll cost me plenty to get help.	1	2	3	4	5
19-M	I have been successful at keeping myself from going back to my old ways of acting when I have conflicts with my partner.	1	2	3	4	5
20-P	If my partner doesn't like the way I act, it's just too bad.	1	2	3	4	5
21-C	Some of what I see and hear about people being abusive seems to apply with me.	1	2	3	4	5
22-P/A	When I feel myself getting upset, I have ways to keep myself from getting into trouble.	1	2	3	4	5
23-C	I'm sick of screwing up my life.	1	2	3	4	5
24-M	I try to talk things out with others so that I don't get into conflicts anymore.	1	2	3	4	5
25-M	I am sure that I will never return to my old ways of treating my partner(s).	1	2	3	4	5
26-P	It's my partner's fault that I act this way.	1	2	3	4	5

27-*	It's okay that I got into trouble because it means that now I'm getting help.	1	2	3	4	5
28-P/A	It's becoming more natural for me to be in control of myself.	1	2	3	4	5
29-P	I'd get help if I had more free time.	1	2	3	4	5
30-P/A	I have a plan for what I do when I feel upset.	1	2	3	4	5
31-*	Recent changes that I have made probably won't last.	1	2	3	4	5
32-C	It's time for me to listen to people telling me that I need help.	1	2	3	4	5
33-M	I know the early cues for when I'm losing control.	1	2	3	4	5
34-P	I need to control my partner.	1	2	3	4	5
35-M	Anyone can talk about changing old ways of acting in relationships. I am actually doing it.	1	2	3	4	5

36. Please check the box for the description that best describes where you think you are, today, in your efforts to change the way you behave with your partner.

(Check only one box)

[ ]   I am not really making any changes.

[ ]   I am thinking about making changes in the future.

[ ]   I am getting ready to make changes or I have made some changes already.

[ ]   I have made some important changes and I have more to do.

[ ]   I have made the changes I needed to make and now I have to keep up the good work.

SAFE AT HOME SCORE SHEET

NOTE: For each item, write your rating on the left underline and the Reverse Code on the underline to the right.

In other words, Reverse Code for 1 = 5, 2 = 4, 3 = 3, 4 = 2, 5 = 1.

Only the Reverse Code scores will be totaled at the end.

P = Precontemplation Stage
C = Contemplation Stage
P/A = Preparation/Action Stage
M = Maintenance

P Reverse ↓	C Reverse ↓	P/A Reverse ↓	M Reverse ↓
Item # 5 Score ___ ___	Item # 1 Score ___ ___	Item # 3 Score ___ ___	Item # 2 Score ___ ___
Item # 11 Score ___ ___	Item # 4 Score ___ ___	Item # 6 Score ___ ___	Item # 16 Score ___ ___
Item # 14 Score ___ ___	Item # 9 Score ___ ___	Item # 12 Score ___ ___	Item # 19 Score ___ ___
Item # 18 Score ___ ___	Item #10 Score ___ ___	Item # 15 Score ___ ___	Item # 24 Score ___ ___
Item # 20 Score ___ ___	Item #13 Score ___ ___	Item # 22 Score ___ ___	Item # 25 Score ___ ___
Item # 26 Score ___ ___	Item #17 Score ___ ___	Item # 28 Score ___ ___	Item # 33 Score ___ ___
Item # 29 Score ___ ___	Item #21 Score ___ ___	Item # 30 Score ___ ___	Item # 35 Score ___ ___
Item # 34 Score ___ ___	Item #23 Score ___ ___		
	Item #32 Score ___ ___		

Total: (REVERSE ONLY) _____
/8 = ___.___
Average for P

Total: (REVERSE ONLY) _____
/9 = ___.___
Average for C

Total: (REVERSE ONLY) _____
/7 = ___.___
Average for P/A

Total: (REVERSE ONLY) _____
/7 = ___.___
Average for M

SCORING: For each column, total the Reverse Code scores, then divide by the number listed in the rows above. You will end up with an average score for each column.

Precontemplation Stage (P): Client denies or minimizes having an anger/aggression problem and has no intention of changing.

Contemplation Stage (C): Client is thinking about changing but has no specific plans.

Preparation Stage (P/A): Client is preparing for change, or actually implementing a change strategy.

Maintenance (M): Client is sustaining the changes previously made.

The average score for each column reflects your scores on the categories above (Precontemplation, Contemplation, etc.)—but the only number that matters is the following:

Overall Readiness to Change: C _____ + P/A _____ − P _____ = _____

Mean Scores (Based on male and female domestic violence clients)

	Male	Female
P	20.37/8 = 2.55 (SD = 0.50)	19.40/8 = 2.43 (SD = 0.63)
C	34.16/9 = 3.80 (SD = 0.83)	34.65/9 = 3.85 (SD = 0.73)
P/A	28.36/7 = 4.05 (SD = 0.54)	29.47/7 = 4.21 (SD = 0.59)
M	28.66/7 = 4.09 (SD = 0.63)	29.50/7 = 4.21 (SD = 0.90)

Overall Readiness to Change

Male Average = **5.30**   Female Average = **5.63**

This Overall Readiness to Change score measures how motivated you currently are to let go of aggressive attitudes and behaviors, learn alternatives, take responsibility, and grow as a person.

Scores above the mean indicate higher than average current Overall Readiness to Change.

Scores below the mean indicate lower than average current Overall Readiness to Change.

For more information: Sielski, C., Begun, A., & Hamel, J. (2015). Expanding knowledge concerning the Safe at Home instruments for assessing readiness-to-change among individuals in batterer treatment. Partner Abuse, 6(3), 255-272.

THE FIVE STAGES OF CHANGE

◆ Handout

Researchers have found that anyone who makes a successful decision to change something that is not working in his or her life goes through a series of stages. This is true for smoking, dieting, drugs and alcohol, gambling, aggressive behavior, and so on.

Everybody who comes into our program enters at their own stage of change. It helps us and it will help you to understand what your stage is—and to notice at various points in your program if there are any changes.

If you do notice movement in these stages, it is valuable to figure out how that happened. Usually something clicks—or the problems reach a breaking point and you decide you really have to move forward.

Here are the classic stages—maybe you can identify even more:

1: PRECONTEMPLATION

I don't have a problem with aggression—so I have no interest in changing my behavior.

2: CONTEMPLATION

I realize I might have a problem with aggression—but I'm not sure I want to do anything about it yet. Maybe later.

3: PREPARATION (or DETERMINATION)

I know now that I have a problem with aggression—and I have to do something about this so I can have a better life and better relationships.

4: ACTION

I realize now that my abusive behavior is unacceptable and I will not allow myself to return to it. I am committing myself to groups, therapy, spiritual guidance, books, and good people—anything to help me make these changes.

5: MAINTENANCE

I realize that it's going to take a lot of work, over a long period of time, to maintain these changes and keep growing. I have to surround myself with the right people and watch carefully for warning signs that I might be slipping.

MAKING CHANGES, PROS AND CONS

◆ Handout

Whenever we think about keeping an old behavior or changing it, it helps to weight the pros and cons—then come to an intelligent decision. Try this with your anger/aggression.

GOOD Things About Anger/Aggression	GOOD Things About Changing Anger/Aggression
NOT-GOOD Things About Anger/Aggression	NOT-GOOD Things About Changing Anger/Aggression

SESSION 25 HOMEWORK

Handout

MAKING CHANGES, PROS AND CONS

If you did not do this in the group session, fill in the blanks on this chart about the pros and cons.
    If you did this in the group, pick out another behavior and apply the model to that.

GOOD Things About Anger/Aggression	GOOD Things About Changing Anger/Aggression
NOT-GOOD Things About Anger/Aggression	NOT-GOOD Things About Changing Anger/Aggression

THE PREVENTION PLAN

◆ Handout

Purpose: To prepare you for future situations when you might be tempted to behave destructively to yourself and/or others.

STEP 2, Cue or Trigger (What could set you off?):

STEP 3, Coping Strategies:

1. **SCARE YOURSELF IMAGE—Example:** Remember the damage to people you love, remember the consequences when you have made mistakes in the past, and so on. What scary image would have an impact on you?

2. **SELF-TALK—Example:** *This isn't worth it. Nobody's perfect. I want to keep my life together.* What would that be for you?

3. **RELAXATION/DISTRACTION—Example:** Deep breathing, listening to music, working out, cleaning up the kitchen, and so on. What would work for you?

4. **FRIENDS/ALLIES—Example:** Call a friend, crisis line, therapist, sponsor, or family member. Who would that be for you?

STEP 1, Behavior I Do *Not* Want to Do (be specific):

_____

_____

SESSION 26 HOMEWORK

◆ Handout

If you *did not* get the chance to work on the Prevention Plan in the group session, prepare one of your own.

If you *did* get the chance to work on the Prevention Plan in the group session, prepare one for another situation and behavior you want to manage.

NOTES

NOTES

NOTES

NOTES

NOTES

NOTES

NOTES

NOTES

NOTES

NOTES